The Hindu Phenomenon

The Hindu Phenomenon

Girilal Jain

UBS Publishers' Distributors Ltd.

New Delhi ● Bombay ● Bangalore ● Madras ●
Calcutta ● Patna ● Kanpur ● London

UBS Publishers' Distributors Ltd.
5 Ansari Road, New Delhi-110 002
Bombay Bangalore Madras
Calcutta Patna Kanpur London

First Published 1994
First Reprint 1994
Second Reprint 1994

Cover Design : UBS Art Studio
Photo : Courtesy *The Observer Group*

Designed & Typeset at UBSPD in 11 pt New Century Schoolbook
Printed at Rajkamal Electric Press, Delhi

Editor's Note

G irilal Jain belonged to that minority of Indian intellectuals who welcomed the movement for the Ram temple as part of the process of Hindu self-renewal and self-affirmation. The rise of Hindus, he argued, was a phenomenon that began 200 years ago with the consolidation of the British Raj and the disarming of the local populace. This produced a fundamental shift in the power balance between Hindus and Muslims which has not been reversed since, though it led to the partition of the country in 1947. Every important Hindu leader from Rammohan Roy to Mahatma Gandhi and Jawaharlal Nehru has made his contribution to the Hindu resurgence. The Ramjanambhoomi movement was only the latest manifestation of this phenomenon, its importance being that it had placed the issue of the civilizational base of Indian nationalism at the centre of the country's political agenda.

Girilal Jain believed that the political-economic order that Jawarharlal Nehru had fashioned was as much in the throes of death as its progenitor, the Marxist-Leninist-Stalinist order. Two major planks of this order, secularism and socialism, had lost much of their old glitter while the third, non-alignment, had become redundant. By the same token, re-Hinduization of the country's political domain had begun.

It was not an accident that the battle between aroused Hindus and the Indian state had been joined on the question of the Ram temple. For Ram was the exemplar *par excellence* for the Hindu public domain. In historic terms, therefore, the proposed temple was another step towards that goal. The proper English translation of 'Hindu *rashtra*' would be 'Hindu polity' and *not* 'Hindu nation'.

The concept of nation was, in fact, Girilal Jain argued, alien to the Hindu temperament and genius. It was essentially Semitic in character, even if it arose in western Europe in the eighteenth century when it had successfully shaken off the Church's stranglehold. For, like Christianity and Islam, it too emphasized the exclusion of those who did not belong to the charmed circle (territorial, linguistic or ethnic) as much as it emphasized the inclusion of those who fell within the circle.

By contrast, the essential spirit of Hinduism was inclusivist, and not exclusivist by definition. Such a spirit must seek to abolish and not build boundaries. That is why he held that the Hindus could not sustain an anti-Muslim feeling except temporarily and, that too, under provocation.

In that sense, Girilal Jain argued, the Hindu fight was not with Muslims; the fight was between Hindus anxious to renew themselves in the spirit of their civilization, and the state and the intellectual class trapped in the debris the British managed to bury us under before they left: "The proponents of the Western ideology are using Muslims as auxiliaries and it is a pity Muslim 'leaders' are allowing themselves to be so used."

Girilal Jain had worked out the broad framework of this project and commenced work on the draft when he fell fatally ill in June 1993. The book has been completed on the basis of his draft, notes and recent writings. Despite all its shortcomings I believe the end result is a fairly accurate statement of his position though, of necessity, it has been stated briefly.

I am grateful to *The Times of India, The Sunday Mail,* and *The Observer* group of publications for permission to use material published in their columns. I would also like to thank Mr. Shamlal, Mr. Inder Malhtora, Mr. Dileep Padgaonkar, Mr. Swapan Dasgupta, Mr. Arun Shourie, Mr. Jagmohan, Mr. Ram Swarup, Mr. Sita Ram Goel and Mr. Gopal Krishna, all friends and colleagues of my father, for their comments and suggestions on the work. I am only too conscious that the responsibility for the shortcomings is entirely mine.

Meenakshi Jain

Contents

Contents

1

The Civilizational Perspective

I must say at the outset that I think in terms which are different from the ones that have dominated the public discourse in our country for a century and longer. I think in terms of *civilizations*, and not *territorial states*. It is not that I do not believe in the validity of the concept of the nation-state as an organizing principle in the economic and political field. I do. But I do not regard it as adequate for defining the nature of our enterprise and therefore the obligation of our state which must flow from a definition of its nature. Indeed, I believe that it is our failure to view ourselves as a civilization and to formulate the tasks for our state accordingly that lies behind many of the problems we face.

As I said at the outset, I think in terms of civilizations and not of nations or territorial states. This is a relatively new development in my life and, to be candid, I do not believe it would have crystallized to the extent it has if the Vishwa Hindu Parishad's (VHP) campaign on the Ramjanambhoomi temple in Ayodhya had not acquired the sweep it had by the time of the *shilanyas* in 1989; if this sweep had not got translated into support for the Bharatiya Janata Party (BJP) in the elections that followed the *shilanyas*; if the BJP had not, as a result, become a significant factor in Indian politics, and, finally, if the popular response to L.K. Advani's *rath yatra* had not been as overwhelming as in fact it turned out to be.

Success, as the saying goes, has many fathers and failure none. But there is a difference between what we call opportunism and willingness to recognize a significant change, especially a change that promises to mark the end of an epoch and the beginning of a new one. I am persuaded that we are witnessing a change of that order in India.

So, as I view the scene, it is no longer particularly relevant to debate whether Hindu *rashtra* is desirable or not, though many of us, mired as we human beings mostly are in modes of thought which have had their day, will continue to engage in this exercise. It has been firmly and finally put on the agenda, though, again many of us would try hard to avoid this recognition because, more often than not, wish is the father of thought for most of us. The pertinent question now is the speed with which this possibility is likely to be realized.

I for one do not regard speculation regarding the time frame to be in order. As a Hindu I believe in the ineluctable power of the time spirit: *Mahakala* will deliver on time – neither earlier nor later. What is material is that the country is well set on that road, and while there may be, indeed there shall be, setbacks, these will be temporary. History zigzags; it never moves in a straight line. But it moves, and according to a pattern.

An epochal change, it is hardly necessary for me to point out, cannot take place unless the existing order has more or less exhausted its beneficial potentialities, and the new order has been in the making for quite some time. Unknown to us and invisible to us, the two processes are more or less simultaneous. This has been the case in India, as I hope to be able to show. The subject is extremely complex and I cannot possibly do anything

like justice to it for a variety of reasons. This would have
been the case even if I was concerned only with the post-
independence period, or the freedom movement. But I am
concerned with a whole millennium. So you can imagine
the difficulties I face in working out and presenting a
theory which is reasonably coherent, intelligible and
acceptable. Before I proceed further, I might add that in
such a framework, there is, at the intellectual level, not
much scope for moral judgement and indignation, though
all that is, of course, valid at the political level.

Why do I think in terms of a whole millennium which,
on the face of it, is fragmented at so many points? My
reason is simple. The beginning of the millennium
witnessed the beginning of the assault on Hindu India
and as we approach its end, we can clearly see the
approach of the end of that assault. Only on a superficial,
so-called rational, view can it be regarded as an accident
that the millennium which began with the destruction of
hundreds and thousands of our temples should be
drawing towards a close amidst an unprecedented
upsurge on the question of the construction of a Ram
temple at a site millions of ordinary Hindus regard as the
avatar's *janambhoomi*.

For me as an analyst, the condemnation of the
campaign in favour of the temple as Hindu 'communalism',
'obscurantism', 'relapse into medievalism' and 'fascism' is
as besides the point as condemnation of the destruction
of Hindu temples, including the famous Somnath, by
Mahmud Ghaznavi at the beginning of the eleventh
century. As a Hindu, I, of course, welcome the former and
feel saddened by the memory of the latter. But analysis
is a different matter altogether. It has to be clinical in
its rigour. By that yardstick, the first is an expression of
Hindu resurgence and the second of the second Islamic
explosion centred on Central Asia, as the first was centred
on Arabia.

Religious-civilizational explosions are like floods and earthquakes. Only in retrospect do their adherents and proponents look for and offer justification for them. When they take place, they are their own justification, or condemnation for victims. This was clearly true of the first Islamic wave in the seventh and eighth centuries, which saw the beginning of the attack on the frontiers of our civilization in Afghanistan, Eastern Iran, Baluchistan, and Sind, and this was equally true of the second Turkic Islamic wave which overtook us precisely because our defences on the border had finally given way after three to four centuries of bitter fight.

In parenthesis, I might mention that Arab Islam was as much a victim of this Turkic Islamic explosion as Hindu India. Indeed, for all practical purposes, the Turks took over the Abbasid caliphate in Baghdad by the middle of the tenth century, that is long before Mahmud Ghaznavi began his raids into India proper. The sack of Baghdad in 1258 was only the culmination of a process that had been on for well over three centuries; in fact, close to four.

It will be outside the scope of this discussion for me to go into the state of India at that time and the nature of the Indian response. Even so, it is necessary to make a couple of points in passing because a distorted perspective has come to dominate our thinking in this regard. India, of course, could not mobilize against Mahmud Ghaznavi and subsequent invaders the kind of vigorous response Chandragupta Maurya had after the raid by Alexander the Great in the fourth century B.C., but this was primarily because the centre of political power had moved from North India, which had to bear the brunt of Muslim invasions, to the Deccan and the south. It is really a shame that so few Hindus are alive to the achievements of the Rashtrakuta, Satvāhan, Chola and Vijaynagar empires. This applies as much to those who rejoice in the Rajput resistance, followed by the Maratha and Sikh resistance, as to those who take pride in the 'glory' of the Mughal empire.

It would also be in order to emphasize that the Hindu resistance to Muslim invasions, conquests and rule was truly heroic, both in fact and in spirit. The first aspect is by now well recognized and need not therefore detain us.[1]* The latter aspect has, however, not received much attention at the hands of historians and, therefore, needs to be specially emphasized.

The Bhakti movement was doubtless part of the Hindu response to Muslim rule. But it is a travesty of the truth to suggest, as is done by any number of Hindu intellectuals, that it represented an attempt to produce a synthesis between Hinduism and Islam. If anything, it was an attempt, even if unconscious, to disarm Islam with the help of a popular movement which clearly demonstrated that equality before God was as much part of Hinduism as it was of Islam. The Bhakti movement was a form of resistance and not an attempt at synthesis or compromise.

Many Hindu intellectuals are just not able to comprehend the fact that there is no human aspiration or experience which lies outside the range of Hinduism; it provides for even demon-Gods. In contrast, all religions are in the nature of sects, though they cannot be so defined because of their insistence on their separateness and, indeed, hostility to Hinduism.

The point I wish particularly to underscore is, however, different; which is that when Hindus fought and lost, they did not throw up prophets of woe and doom; they did not bemoan that their Gods had let them down because they had been 'disloyal' to them. Hindus are

---

* For further details, please see 'Notes and References' in all following cases.

perhaps unique in this respect. That is perhaps why the
well-known British historian Elliot wondered why Hindus
had not left any account which could enable us to gauge
the traumatic impact Muslim conquests and rule had on
them. (Incidentally, one such account entitled *Kanhadade
Prabandha* by the Jain Muni Padmanabha written in the
fifteenth century regarding the fight for the Jalore fort
is available, and the muni-poet praises Muslim valour as
he praises Hindu valour. An English translation of this
unique document, with an introduction and annotation
by V.S. Bhatnagar, has recently been published.)[2]

A large number of Hindus, of course, cooperated with
Muslim rulers and millions even got converted to Islam.
It is important to know, even in retrospect, how Islam
spread. But, for one thing, the distinction that is often
made between conversion by force (sword), temptation
(favours by the court) and persuasion (influence of pious
Sufis) is rather arbitrary because all three factors
operated in conjunction with one another; and, for
another, the more critical point for us is that by the time
the Mughal empire went into decline in the early
eighteenth century, a kind of stalemate had been reached,
with neither the Hindus nor the Muslims able to
dominate India as a whole. It was in this context that
the British came to rule over India.

We can speculate on the likely course of events in case
the British had not arrived on the scene. Personally, I do
not, as a rule, engage in such speculation. I regard it as
futile. We have to interpret facts as they came to obtain
on the ground, for whatever reason. In such an approach,
it is relevant to discuss the factors behind a particular
development. But it is far more pertinent to concentrate
on the consequences. That is what, in any case, I propose
to do, of course, in relation to my central proposition that
we are set on the path to Hindu *rashtra*. The consequences of the Raj form a vast and complex subject. If,

however, it is not possible for us to deal with it in a meaningful manner here, it is also not urgent.

It is a commonplace that the Raj was very different from Muslim rule. Two differences have been spotlighted by any number of historians and commentators. They have said that the British remained foreigners, while Muslim invaders and immigrants made India their home, and that the British drained India of its wealth which Muslim rulers did not because the latter settled down here for good.

For me, however, there is a third difference which is of critical importance. This difference is that the British did not come to India — and did not rule over India — as part of a proselytizing enterprise in the religious realm. Indeed, it was with great reluctance that the authorities in Calcutta, acting on behalf of the East India Company, yielded to the pressure from London to allow Christian missionaries to enter India and engage in proselytization. In the absence of backing by the state, however, the Christian missionaries could achieve only a pretty limited measure of success and, that too, largely among weaker sections of society, which could be tempted and manipulated. This absence of a direct link between the state and the Church offered great relief to Hindus and ensured their survival in freedom, and, therefore, held out the prospect of Hindu self-affirmation. It is my contention that a process of self-affirmation, in fact, began with the establishment and consolidation of British rule. I view Raja Rammohan Roy and other reformers as much in that light as men such as Ramakrishna Parmahansa, Swami Vivekanand, Sri Aurobindo and Maharishi Raman.

The British ruled over India as representatives of Western civilization. Christianity was doubtless a major constituent of that civilization. But with Renaissance in the fifteenth century and Enlightenment in the eighteenth, Christianity ceased to be its 'informing principle'. The Graeco-Roman heritage took its place. This heritage was pagan; it provided for plurality in every sphere of human activity; and it therefore promoted acceptance of a relativist approach. As such, Hinduism could easily come to terms with it and, in fact, *accommodate* it. And precisely for the same reason, Islam could not come to terms with it. By virtue of being a legatee of Western civilization (rooted at least as much in an ancient pagan civilization, similar to India's, if not India's sister or daughter via Egypt, as in Christianity), the Raj constituted a challenge to Islam, while it served as a stimulus to Hindus for self-discovery and recovery.

As it happened, at the beginning of the nineteenth century, some British and other European scholars were launched on a search for the origins of their civilization. In this search they discovered links not only between Latin, Greek, German, English and French within Europe, but also between classical European languages, that is, Latin and Greek, and Sanskrit and the original language of Zend Avesta. This again is a long and complex story which certainly does not run in a straight line. But it would suffice for our purpose to note that the efforts of Orientalists – Sir William Jones clearly the most outstanding among them in the latter part of the eighteenth century which was of critical importance by virtue of its being the formative period for the Raj as well as for Hindu India in the new context – restored to Hindus confidence in their heritage. This confidence has in a fundamental sense, not been shaken since, whatever else might have happened in between. And, needless to add, no similar advantage flowed to Islam in India, or for that matter anywhere else, from the British Raj, or any other Western empire, or contact.

The British, of course, did not come to India primarily as representatives of Western civilization; they came principally as traders and settled down as rulers. The consequences of the first role have been extensively discussed and I have not much to add to the broad consensus that this led to our deindustrialization and, therefore, impoverishment. The same is largely true of other consequences of their rule. Here, too, a broad consensus obtains. Even so I would draw attention to a couple of points which, in my opinion, have not received the attention they deserve.

First, the British disarmed us, for the first time in history. Till the consolidation of British power in India in 1858, the Indian peasantry was armed. According to the Ain-i-Akbari, four and a half million armed men were available for military service in North India in the sixteenth century and possibly a similar number below the Vindhyas, judging by the fact that the Vijaynagar empire could field up to one million soldiers. This subject has not been discussed much. But the gap in this field has been ably filled by a recent publication – Dirk H.A. Kolff's *Naukar, Rajput and Sepoy*.[3] Broadly, it makes the points that the Indian peasantry in modern Uttar Pradesh, Bihar and Madhya Pradesh (which is the area of Kolff's research) was armed; that a substantial labour market existed; that there was no dearth of employment opportunities for would-be soldiers; that these recruits came from all strata of society including the lowest in ritual terms; that there was no discrimination in the recruitment and treatment of soldiers of any kind on the basis of caste; indeed, that caste is a modern ideology inasmuch as it restricts mobility because from the fourteenth to the eighteenth century Rajput status was accessible to soldiers; and that a Hindu soldier had more than one identity.

Clearly, so dramatic a development as the disarming of a people used to carrying and wielding weapons could not but have had major consequences. Clearly this issue deserves to be studied at length. In the present context, I would wish to underscore the point that the British move affected Muslims more adversely than Hindus for the simple reason that Muslims were more dependent on the use of the sword than Hindus who had successfully maintained their primacy in business even during Mughal rule[4] and had been much quicker to take advantage of the opportunities Western education offered them for entry into professions such as law and government employment.

I am convinced that a significant and fundamental shift took place in the power balance between Hindus and Muslims as a result of the consolidation of the Raj and the disarming of the populace which began in 1818 and was completed in 1858, and that this shift was not reversed by the pro-Muslim change in the official attitude, starting from the 1870s, and the policy of divide and rule, though it led to partition in 1947. Indeed, it could not be reversed.

The British, of course, had no desire to help the re-emergence of Hindus. Indeed, as educated Hindus began to assert claims to equality, demand share in government and resent racist slurs, the British took steps to contain them. But all that is besides the point. The relevant fact is that the Raj made possible the rise of a self-confident Hindu elite on an all-India basis, the like of which had not existed since the beginning of Muslim rule.

Partition was a logical corollary to the rise of Hindus. The British assistance to the Muslim League during the Second World War, however important, only accelerated the pace of events; the alternative to partition, in the shape of continued separate electorates, weightage and special reservations would have been disastrous and though partition did not settle the civilizational contest that began with Muslim rule, it facilitated the task for Hindus since they had now a well-organized and powerful pan-Indian modern state of their own.

These observations will almost certainly be quoted to show that I endorse Muhammad Ali Jinnah's two-nation theory. There is nothing I can do to avoid this risk. For my readers, however, I would emphasize not only that I think in civilizational as distinct from national terms, but also that, by my reckoning, Muslims in undivided India could represent only a fragment of Islamic civilization and were, therefore, incapable of becoming a people.

Jinnah could call Indian nationalism, as espoused by the Indian National Congress, 'Hindu nationalism' on the ground that the Congress was a Hindu body, which it was, by virtue of its ethos if not by that of its ideology and composition, and pit 'Muslim nationalism' against it. But he could not possibly overcome the obstinate fact that Islam, on the one hand, does not admit of nationalism and, on the other, does not help overcome local and even tribal loyalties.

Thus, while Jinnah could bring Muslims together on an anti-Hindu platform and force the country's partition, he could not lay the foundations of a Pakistani nation. It is not surprising that Pakistan continues to 'define' itself in anti-India and anti-Hindu terms. It could not possibly overcome its essentially transient character and disruptive role and it has not. The military muscle it has acquired, thanks to US bounty and Soviet stupidity, has inevitably increased its capacity for mischief but not its ability to define itself in terms of itself.

To return to the subject under discussion, independence, accompanied by partition, removed two constraints – British control and Muslim intransigence – blocking our march forward and, in objective terms, therefore, paved the way for the re-emergence of Hindu India in civilizational, and not just in physical, terms. In physical terms, independent India has been Hindu India. But a Hindu civilizational India has yet to emerge.

As I see it, several obstacles have blocked this process. First, as a rule, without any exception, for decades, to the best of my knowledge, we Hindus have viewed our civilization in parochial terms; even those of us who have related it to other pre-Judaic faiths have not realized that the West has achieved what we are struggling to achieve; that the Europeans, in plain terms, have successfully resurrected and renewed an ancient civilization by way of a series of movements beginning with the Italian Renaissance in the fifteenth century. Instead of seeing it as a sister civilization in view of its emphasis on reason, rule of law and spirit of inquiry, we have condemned the West on the ground that it was materialistic, as if material well-being was not one of the principal concerns of our forefathers.

Secondly, we have taken a territorial and, therefore, a mechanical view and not a civilizational view of ourselves as a people. Thus, by reckoning, we were Indians by virtue of living in a country called India and we were equally justified in calling every inhabitant of the territory Hindu since Muslims named it Hindustan. This theory is reflected in the writings and utterances of not only 'secularists', but also BJP leaders. But for this mechanical concept, we could never have accepted the proposition that the Indian state is an impartial arbiter between the two communities. The contrast between the secularist-national position and the Hindu position on this question is sharp.

The secularist-national position is that the Indian state embodies an ideal, and is there to serve it; that while it is a creature of the Constitution, it is above the people; that in our multireligious society, there is no other choice. In the Hindu view, the state has to be an expression of the Hindu ethos and personality. Such a state cannot either discriminate against any religious group or seek to impose a uniform pattern on the inhabitants. Indeed, it would feel obliged to look after their well-being and the preservation of their ways of life. But the state would see itself as an instrument for the promotion of Hindu civilization.

The final point that I wish to make here is that we opted for the policy of non-alignment with a visible anti-Western bias because we took a parochial view of our civilization and wrongly defined the nature of the state in independent India. Pandit Nehru saw himself as an arbiter between rival camps in the cold war, in disregard of the horror that was communism, just as he saw himself as an arbiter between Hindus and Muslims within the country. Obviously, the cost on both counts has been pretty heavy. If non-alignment has meant the isolation of India from true centres of power in our era, the concept of secularism has meant the moral disarmament of Hindus. Pakistan and China could not have posed the kind of threat they have to our security if we had made common cause with the West and the Muslim problem would not have remained wholly unresolved if we had not misdefined the nature of the Indian state.

2

A Unique Phenomenon

The first point that needs to be emphasized in a meaningful discussion of Hindu nationalism is that it is something altogether different from other types of nationalisms, with the possible exception of the Chinese about which it is premature to say anything definite since the Chinese people have yet to recover their capacity to shape their future in accordance with their civilization and genius. The reason is simple. The Hindu civilization, which is the basis of Hindu nationalism, is different from any other living civilization, again with the partial exception of the Chinese. Even when the uniqueness of our civilization is accepted, it is sought to be annulled for all practical purposes, by giving it the label 'Hinduism' and equating it with other religions. The tragedy is that most educated Hindus have themselves fallen prey to this semantic confusion. Thus they describe themselves as one community among others. It follows that we should shun the term 'Hinduism'; but that is not a practical proposition.

What we can, however, do is emphasize again and again that *Hinduism is not a religion*. René Guenon, one of the best-known European traditionalist authors on various civilizations, writes in his book *Introduction to the Study of the Hindu Doctrines*: "...the term 'religion' is difficult to apply strictly outside the group formed by Judaism, Christianity and Islam, which goes to prove the specifically Jewish origin of the idea that the word now expresses."[1] He adds: "In India we are in the presence of a tradition which is purely metaphysical in its essence.... A fact which stands out much more clearly here than in the Islamic tradition, chiefly owing to the absence of the religious point of view, ...is the complete subordination of the various particular orders relatively to metaphysics, that is to say relatively to the realm of universal principles."[2]

Hinduism has been called a confederation of religions by apologists as well as detractors. That definition cannot, and does not, do justice to the spirit of the Hindu people. For, religion as such is a Semitic enterprise. It must, by definition, draw a boundary between the believer and the unbeliever; the chosen and the rejected; the blessed and the damned; the truly faithful and the heretic. It must divide. It just cannot do otherwise unless it comes to be tempered by other influences, as Christianity has been tempered gradually by the upsurge of the Graeco-Roman civilization since the Renaissance in Europe in the fifteenth century. That was a sister civilization to ours. That is why its coming in via British rule could help stimulate and renew Hindu civilization despite its Christian undertones and attempts at proselytization by the missionaries.

Hindus accept no divisions between the believer and the unbeliever. Every path leads to Him (God or Reality); there can be as many paths to Him as the number of human, in fact, sentient, beings. For, every being is differently constituted, with different capacities and needs, and can follow only a path appropriate to him or her. As such, Hindus can have no difficulty in accepting the legitimacy of Christianity and Islam for their adherents, though for themselves they cannot possibly accept either Christ as the only son of God, or Mohammed as the seal of prophecy and the Koran as the immutable word of God to be taken literally. Indeed, the prophetic tradition is alien to Hinduism. An avatar (incarnation of God) is not a Hindu variant of the .prophet. His actions and sayings are not immune to interpretation and, in fact, to disregard and rejection.

Hinduism provides for the ultimate Truth but not for a final and last statement of that Truth. So, we cannot have either *the* son of God, or *the* last messenger of God, or *the* final revelation. Indeed, in our civilization, when we project a *nayak*, we also project a *priti-nayak*, the *nayak's* opposite.

It is not an accident that Hindus do not bury their dead; they cremate them; they do so primarily because they do not believe in resurrection which, needless to add, is the source of the belief in the possibility of a religious-cultural revival. It is a popular saying among Hindus that the soul sheds the body just as a snake sheds its skin to take on a new one.

Hinduism provides for self-renewal, even if Hindus as such have not been able to make effective use of the built-in mechanism for change for centuries. The concept of *Kalabrahma* or *Kaladharma* is central to the Hindu way of thinking. It accepts explicitly the inevitability of change with the passage of time. The past is not superseded but is modified according to the demands of the spirit of the times, determined, in the traditional Indian view, by the cosmic movement of planets. Thus the Vedas are followed by the Upanishads and these by the Epics and the Puranas; nothing is final.

The *siddha* tradition is as old as Hinduism; Goraknath, to whom we attribute the Tantric tradition was himself the 84th and the last in the line of master *siddhas*. All in the line engaged in the same search for experience of

Reality and Truth but everyone sought to communicate it in the spirit of the time in which he lived. The same is true of the 24 Jain Tirthankaras and 24 Buddhas. In our times we have the case of the Sikh Gurus – the nine following Guru Nanak embodying the same spirit and engaging in the same search and yet communicating it in different forms. Masters such as Ramakrishna Parmahansa, Sri Aurobindo and Maharishi Raman too sought to renew old traditions. Sri Aurobindo even wrote mostly in the English language. Such a civilization just cannot admit of revivalism.

This catholicity of outlook is, of course, not a peculiarity of Hindus. Other ancient civilizations -- Mesopotamian, Babylonian, Egyptian, Iranian, Minoan, Greek, Celtic, Chinese, Mayan and Aztec – are known to have been informed by a similar spirit. None of them is believed to have engaged in proselytization and heresy hunting. Both these began with Yahweh's contract with Moses with the dual proclamation of a chosen people and a jealous God, and achieved their acme under Christianity and Islam since Judaism came to be identified with a specific racial group and not only ceased to be a proselytizing faith but instead became a persecuted one. (With the exception of a brief respite after the Babylonian captivity in the sixth century B.C., when Jews are known to have lost the memory of even their language, they have faced persecution throughout their history, culminating in Hitler's 'final solution' in which six million Jews are known to have been murdered.)

In fact, Moses, real or mythical, marks a radical departure from all previous spiritual traditions. Christian and Muslim writers have argued that uncompromising monotheism, as first propounded by Moses, represents a higher stage in the evolution of religion. But that is a different matter which can be allowed to rest for the time being. What is important to emphasize right now is that along with the doctrine of uncompromising monotheism, heresy hunting, proselytization and holy wars became integral parts of Semitic religions.

The proselytizing impetus in Christianity and Islam is far from exhausted even in this secular age, as is evident from their massive campaigns, especially in Africa, and from the persecution of Muslim 'heretics' such as the Ahmadiyas in Pakistan and Bahais in Iran and of non-Muslim peoples in Sudan. The details are blood-chilling.

Nazism, fascism and communism have been expressions of the same Semitic spirit in the secular realm. They too divided human beings into friends and foes and looked for 'dissidents' in their own ranks. Indeed, it would not be too wide off the mark to say that the Christian passion for proselytization got diverted into these 'ideological' channels in our century leading to one tragedy after another, ironically for Christians. While it is terrible that six million Jews should have died in Nazi gas chambers, it should be remembered that something like 100 million Christians perished as a result of Nazism and communism in concentration camps and during the Second World War.

While other people have, in the past, shared a similar catholicity of outlook, Hindus can claim two unique achievements which set them apart. Hindus alone developed yogic techniques on a regular scientific basis which any interested person can study and practice, preferably under the guidance of a guru (preceptor), according to his capacity and commitment. This fact is recognized by leading authorities on yoga the world over. Shamanism is not yoga, as Mircea Eliade, a leading authority on comparative religion, recognizes. And it might be added that yoga is the basis of Hindu spirituality. Equally important, Hindus alone have been able to preserve an unbroken link with the past and a comprehensive corpus of ancient knowledge in all branches of human activity.

The links with the past have, in many respects, degenerated into mere rituals and superstitious practices in the absence of a living tradition of knowledge and experimentation, which once informed the rituals and other practices. Similarly, ancient texts have often been distorted through literalist interpretations, resulting partly from dramatic changes in language, as from Vedic Sanskrit to classical Sanskrit, for instance, and partly from the same absence of a living tradition of knowledge and experimentation. Both these difficulties are now being overcome to an extent. The hold of rituals has declined and the ancient texts have begun to be better understood. But the process is far from being sufficiently advanced to permit us to speak of a renewal of the Hindu civilization.

Texts such as the Vedas and Upanishads are not intellectual constructs like Western philosophy; they are statements of spiritual experience and guides to that experience. Since the key to them in the shape of yogic techniques survives, it can give master practitioners access to our past in a manner and on a scale which is unique to us. Indeed, such fragmentary texts as survive from other old civilizations are also best approached via the Hindu route. There is a universality about ancient civilizations which is no less remarkable than the globalization of today. So it is logical that we approach the unknown through the known.

It may be recalled that it was in pursuit of yogic *sadhana,* independently of access to Vedic knowledge at that stage, that Sri Aurobindo acquired the key which enabled him to interpret the Vedas in their pristine spirit. He had experiences similar to those described in the Vedas by the great rishis and that enabled him to know what the *slokas,* in fact, meant. Sri Aurobindo writes in his book *On the Vedas*:

> My first contact with Vedic thought came indirectly
> while pursuing certain lines of self-development in the
> way of Indian Yoga which, without my knowing it,
> were spontaneously covering towards the ancient and
> now unfrequented paths followed by our forefathers.
> At this time began to arise in my mind an
> arrangement of symbolic names attached to certain
> psychological experiences which had begun to
> regularise themselves; and among them came the
> figures of three female energies, Ila, Saraswati,
> Sarama, representing...three out of the four faculties
> of the intuitive reason – revelation, inspiration and
> intuition.[3]

Ramayana and Mahabharata, the great Hindu epics,
too have been interpreted in symbolic terms.[4]

The reference to the continuity of our tradition has
long been a commonplace. At the level of formulation, it
can be traced back to the eighteenth century when
Western scholars began to discover and translate Sanskrit
manuscripts. The reference is legitimate on two counts.
First, the continuity from the time of the Indus Valley
civilization is evident in matters such as dress, means of
transport, and even sculpture. The dancing girl from
Mohenjodaro could, for instance, have been sculpted at
any point in Indian history. Secondly, thanks to its faithful
preservation, above all by Brahmins, we have access to
an unbelievable amount of ancient knowledge in a wide
variety of fields. Much of what must have been produced
has doubtless perished; but what is left is enormous.

These points need to be emphasized because the continuity of practices, even if routinized, and the availability
of an enormous corpus of ancient knowledge make it
possible for us to engage in a search for self-renewal and
self-affirmation in our own terms. This is not open to

peoples of other ancient civilizations because their past
has been obliterated. Ancient Egypt, for instance, is only
a memory to Egyptians. The better educated among them
can, at best, derive pride from the unrivalled pyramids.
The heritage itself means little to them. It certainly does
not arouse among them the desire to reclaim it.

To take up our own case, it is about time we recognize
that we are not a *nation* in the European sense of the
term, that is, we are not a fragment of a civilization
claiming to be a nation on the basis of accidents of history
which is what every major European nation is. We are a
people primarily by virtue of the continuity and coherence
of our civilization which has survived all shocks. And
though inevitably weakened as a result of foreign
invasions, conquests and rule for almost a whole
millennium, it is once again ready to resume its march.

The sources from which the Indian populace came to
be constituted are strangely enough, still a matter of
debate. Theories of Aryan invasion/migration and of pre-
Aryan indigenous Dravidian people and civilization
survive despite the absence of worthwhile evidence. There
can, however, be no question that there had come into
existence within, more or less, the present boundaries of
South Asia a civilization pervasive enough and deep
enough to give rise to a people who can be said to possess
a collective psyche.

Such a civilization existed in India at least on the eve
of the Christian era. Evidence in support of a substantial
Buddhist-Jain presence in Tamil Nadu by the second
century B.C. and of the fusion of the supposedly Aryan-
Dravidian features to produce one homogeneous
civilization is by now well documented.[5]

I am not persuaded of the existence of a separate
Dravida-speaking community in India. I share the views

of the well-known archaeologist, Dr. S.R. Rao, that the
Indus Valley civilization was a Vedic civilization.[6] But I
do not wish to press this viewpoint in this presentation,
though I would like to make two points in passing.

First, at the heart of the Aryan-Dravidian theory lies
the Western scholarly definition of 'distinct' speech
communities in Central Asia, accepted by them as the
nursery of races and nations. On their own findings,
however, these 'distinct' communities are not all that
distinct after all. Indeed, they could not be, in view of
their close proximity, on the reckoning of Western scholars
themselves. Secondly, if northern Iran and Afghanistan
are recognized to be parts of Central Asia, as they are, it
is logical to extend the definition to include the northern-
western part of India now Pakistan. That would give
Vedic Sanskrit, or a possible earlier version of it, the
status it may well deserve, but has been denied.

It is in any case beyond dispute that there arose in
South Asia a civilization so homogeneous that it is
difficult to locate a tradition, or a folklore, in any locality
in South Asia in any Indian language which is not related
to a similar tradition or folklore in other parts of the land
in other languages. In fact, there is a remarkable
continuity between classical traditions, widely regarded
as the handiwork of the upper strata, especially
Brahmins, and folklore, which, on the other hand, is said
to be the creation of ordinary people. Again, there is no
local or folk tradition which is not found in the Sanskritic-
Brahminic tradition.

As Ananda K. Coomaraswamy correctly pointed out,
folklore in India should not be contrasted with the
classical traditions, as it is in Europe. "Whereas in Europe
folk and classical traditions are separate, in India they
share a common base.... In fact, these terms represent
only different (the local and pan-Indian) expressions of
the same tradition, not different traditions". [See Stuart

H. Blackburn and A.K. Ramanujan (eds.), *Another Harmony: New Essays on the Folklore of India*.][7] This unity covered not only 'Dravida' India, if indeed a distinct Dravida speech community existed, but also tribal India. We have a pretty good idea now of the interaction between tribal India and Hindu India in the rise of Gods, for example.

Orissa is ideal for studying this phenomenon for a variety of reasons. While it is a distinct geographical unit with a distinct cultural and political history, north-eastern and southern influences have met there and it has been in direct contact with Central and North India through the Mahanadi valley. Its regional tradition has remained relatively unbroken. It was, for instance, able to withstand Muslim conquest till 1568, more than three centuries after much of North and Central India had come under Muslim rule. Finally, Orissa has had a large tribal population; even today tribals account for almost 25 per cent of the total population. The uninterrupted tribal-Hindu continuum finds its lasting manifestation in the Jagannath cult of Puri. "The archaic iconography of the cult images on the one hand and their highest Hindu iconology on the other as well as the existence of former tribals (*daitas*) and Vedic Brahmins amongst its priests are no by means an antithesis, but a splendid regional synthesis of the local and the all-India tradition." [See Anncharlott Eschmann *et al.* (eds.), *The Cult of Jagannath and the Regional Tradition of Orissa*.][8] Interestingly, the very tribes, whose cults have been incorporated, still live as tribal and semi-tribal communities in the region, and Hinduization can be observed "in the making".[9]

To cite another example. The main image of the Khambhesvari temple in Aska (Ganjam) consists of a stone pole – poles and stones normally substitute for images for tribals – which has been anthropomorphized by the addition of a disk as head. The nose and the mouth are slightly carved; the eyes, the protruding tongue, and the nose ornament, are made of gold. "The image of Khambhesvari confers both: the impression of a real Hindu image – whose body and limbs are mostly not to be seen because of the dresses and ornaments – *and* the impression of the pole, whose form is still evident in spite of the dress. It is thus a very happy combination...."[10]

To clinch the issue. The Lingaraja temple in Bhubaneswar, built in the eleventh century, has two classes of priests: Brahmins and a class called Badus who are ranked as Sudras and are said to be of tribal origin. Not only are Badus priests of this important temple; they also remain in the most intimate contact with the deity whose personal attendants they are. Only they are allowed to bathe the Lingaraja and adorn him and at festival time when the god, "represented by his *calanti pratima* [original symbols of the deity], leaves the temple only Badus may carry this movable image. Without them, it is said, the god 'cannot move one step'...."[11]

The temple legends confirm and 'explain' the tribal origin of the cult: "They indicate that the deity was originally under a mango tree...and it was not seen as a *linga* in the first two ages, Satya and Treta. In the Dvapara and Kali ages it revealed itself as *linga*.... The Badus are described by the legend as tribals (*sabaras*) who originally inhabited the place and worshiped the *linga* under the tree".[12]

In view of deliberate attempts in recent decades to project Buddhism and Jainism as separate religions, distinct from Hinduism, it would be in order to deal with them in passing. The attempts have clearly been motivated by the design to separate their followers from the parent body called Hinduism just as Sikhs have been to an extent. Though not to the same extent as in the case of Sikhs, the attempts have succeeded inasmuch as neo-Buddhists and at least some Jains have come to regard themselves as non-Hindus.

In reality, however, Buddhism and Jainism have been no more than movements within the larger body of Hinduism, not significantly different from Lingayats, Saktas or Bhaktas of more recent times. Regardless of whether we call them sects or religions, and in the case of Jains, whether we accept the view that they represent the earliest religion of India or that their first Tirthankar, Adinath, is the same as the Hindu god Shiva, the reality is the constant interaction of the most intimate kind between them and Brahmins. Indeed, individuals, Brahmin by birth, have been leaders in the formulation and propagation of Jainism as well as Buddhism. Narrowness of the spirit, peculiar to Semitic faiths, has been alien to India.

Louis Dumont has dealt with Jainism and Buddhism in his famous work. *Homo Hierarchicus*.[13] Tracing the origins of *ahimsa* and vegetarianism, he says both were originally confined to the renouncer (that is a person who leaves social life to devote himself to his salvation) and forced themselves on Hindu society under the influence of Jainism and Buddhism, "the two great disciplines of salvation":

> After all, how many kinds of spiritual authority were there? Only two: the Brahman and his tradition, the renouncer and his sects. How many factors of initiative and invention? Only one, the renouncer, faced with whom the Brahman was such an effective factor of integration and aggregation that in the long run he almost completely absorbed his rivals. There was rivalry in public opinion between these two sorts of "spirituality", and this by itself can contribute to the explanation of the efforts to go one better, the

hardening of the doctrines as, penetrating into the
social world proper, they were taken up by the
Brahman on his own account. (Let us not forget that
the Kshatriyas have traditionally remained meat-
eaters.) In short, the Brahman would have adopted
vegetarianism so as not to be outdone by the
renouncer qua spiritual leader.[14]

This unity was not ruptured by subsequent invasions
by Scythians, Huns and other groups from Central Asia
till the arrival of Islam, first in Sind in the early eighth
century and, finally, in the Indo-Gangetic plains in the
eleventh century. The pre-Islamic invaders did not
generally penetrate the heartland of Indian civilization
and the Gangetic plains; entering through the north-west,
they moved down south-west via Rajasthan into Gujarat.
Moreover, they were soon absorbed into the Hindu or the
Buddhist tradition, if they did not bear the impress of
these traditions already. Unlike in Europe where they
finally overwhelmed the Roman empire, they made no
lasting impact on India.

The cultural unity we have spoken of would obviously
not have been possible in the absence of a common
language of literary culture. Sanskrit fulfilled that role.
Two views have been expressed about Sanskrit. First,
that it was the language of an Aryan people who came
to India as conquerors and/or migrants from Central Asia
and successfully imposed it on the native peoples.
Secondly, that it was a language which was developed
within India itself as a result of the synthesis of the
languages of various ethnic groups, who were themselves
in the process of becoming merged into one people, and
that this was the reason why there was no popular
resistance to it at any stage.

Clearly, the first is the more widespread view largely
as a result of the work of Western scholars. This is rather

surprising not only for the reason (outlined earlier) that if Central Asia was indeed the nursery of nations and speech communities, these could not be all that different from one another in view of the close proximity in which the peoples involved must have lived. There is another reason for the surprise. Max Mueller, who played a leading role in popularizing philology, the so-called science of languages, denied the existence of an Aryan race. Others have followed him, especially after the disaster of Nazism in Europe. Not many people now accept the theory of a pure race.

One of India's best known linguists, the late Professor Suniti Kumar Chatterjee, has expounded the second viewpoint again and again. He was a scholar in the Western tradition of Orientalism. As such, he accepted the theory of Aryan invasion/migration as well as broadly the dates in respect of Indian history as determined by Western scholars; he rejected dates based on astronomical calculations of events mentioned in the Vedas, epics and Puranas. I have reservations on both these counts; but let that pass and let us discuss Professor Chatterjee's views.

According to Professor Chatterjee, various people of diverse origins – the Austric Nishadas (Kols or Mundas), Dramidas or Dravidians, the Aryans and Kiratas or Mongoloids – began to live together in the well-demarcated geographical area of India three to four thousand years ago. Then began a racial fusion and cultural and linguistic miscegenation among them. In this work of welding together diverse people into one, Brahmin thinkers (mainly of Aryan origin) and the various Aryan language-speaking groups of military adventurers and business classes, always on the move, made the greatest contribution. A cultural ideology, including some social trends and practices and religious notions, became established. This cultural basis, with its Sanskrit name

of *Dharma*, became, at least from the end of the second
millennium B.C. (circa 1500-1000 B.C.), an irresistible force
bringing together, under the guidance of the Brahmin
priestly class, various peoples of India.[15]

What we loosely call Sanskrit, as the vehicle of Hindu
culture, can, with greater accuracy, be described as
Spoken Aryan, as it evolved roughly between 500 B.C. and
A.D. 500. *It included not only classical Sanskrit as it
evolved from Vedic Sanskrit under the impact of Dravidian
and Kol (tribal) speeches but also contemporary Prakrit
or vernacular Aryan dialects (Jain Prakrit, Pali, etc.) and
the mixed Sanskrit and Prakrit of Buddhists (Buddhist
hybrid Sanskrit) and all other speeches within the Aryan
orbit as used from 500 B.C. onwards.* And in the vital
matters of syntax and vocabulary, both classical Sanskrit
and various Prakrits were deeply influenced by Dravidian
and Austric (tribal) languages. "In the evolution of the
Aryan speech, the Dravidians and the Austrics had
almost an equal hand as the original speakers of old Indo-
Aryan."[16]

Further, "Sanskrit looms large behind all Indian
languages, Aryan and non-Aryan. It is inseparable from
Indian history and culture. *Sanskrit* is *India*. The
progressive Unification of the Indian Peoples into a single
Nation can correctly be described as the Sanskritisation
of India."[17]

Just as Sanskrit was to unify diverse groups into one
people with a common culture, Hindavi or Hindi was to
play the same role in the preservation of this cultural
unity. It is not generally known that Hindavi or Hindi was
the successor to Sanskrit as an all-India language from
the ninth century onwards; that it was not limited to
what is now regarded as the Hindi-speaking region; and
that its pan-Indian spread was possible precisely because
like Sanskrit, it did not grow out of one Prakrit. As
scholars have pointed out, Hindi developed, like Romance

languages in Europe, as an exogenous and not as an endogenous language. Viswanath Prasad writes:

> It is generally surmised about the modern Indian languages that each of them must have evolved from some Prakrit or Apabhransa. Some people think the same about Hindi. But in so far as Hindi does not reflect the features and characteristics of any *one* Prakrit or Apabhransa, it does not sound reasonable to think that it has derived from any *one* of them. The fact of the matter is that Hindi has developed, like the European Romance languages, by a process of *sankramana*, and not *vyutkramana*, i.e., as an exogenous language and not as an endogenous language. According to Udyotana Suri's *Kuvalayamala*, there were at least sixteen regional languages and dialects current in the eighth-ninth centuries. In the north, in Panjab, and in the east, in the languages and dialects prevalent between Bihar and Bengal, we notice that although in their spoken form they had local peculiarities, they were nevertheless gradually tending towards a common standard. It is clear from the Apabhransa literature of the eighth to the twelfth centuries that, on account of the particular feature of development mentioned above, the literary language of the time was in a large measure standardized, and in the written form there were not many regional variations. The emergence of Hindi as a common language of literary usage is clearly evident from the Apabhransa literature of the time. The best examples of the exogenous development of the Hindi language and its literature are to be found in the writings of the Siddha poets. There is no doubt that we find the oldest forms of Hindi in those works.

In 1916, after the publication by the late Pandit Haraprasada Shastri of a collection of Siddha poetry under the title *Bauddha Gan o Doha*, various theories

were propounded about the language of that body of
writing. Mr. Shastri himself, and some other scholars,
thought it the earliest form of Bengali. On the other
hand, others discovered in it the old forms of Oriya
or Maithili or Bhojpuri or Magahi.

The truth is that there is a great deal of similarity
in these eastern languages; they are all related to
Magadhi Apabhransa which had not, until then,
developed many variations in its local forms.
Therefore it was easy to discover in the many usages
in these works, the forms or signs of development of
this or that language. But the most important thing
to remember in this connection is that most of these
Siddha works had been written in the famous
universities of Nalanda and Vikramsila, and their
writers mostly belonged to that region. Therefore this
surmise is certainly much strengthened: that their
language must have been some form of the Magadhi
or Magahi prevalent there. With that base the
Siddhas unhesitatingly mixed the standard forms of
western Apabhransa with the current forms of the
adjacent western districts, and thus developed a
literary style in their writings which would help them
reach out and influence a much wider public with
their ideas. Consequently, in that one mirror of writing
it is possible to see reflections of ever so many forms.
In fact, Hindi is the result of just such natural and
voluntary mixtures, whose oldest specimens can be
witnessed in Siddha literature. The late Kashi Prasad
Jayaswal and Rahul Sankrityayana were the first
people who drew attention to these Siddha poets in
terms of the origin and development of Hindi, and to
the fact that through them the early period of Hindi
authentically goes back to the eighth century A.D.
(Quoted in Amrit Rai, *A Divided House: The Origin
and Development of Hindi / Hindavi*.)[18]

As would be obvious from the foregoing quotation, Siddha poets played a critical role in the development of the Hindi language. They represented a revolt against practices which are associated with *vamacara* (esoteric occult practices of the *mantra* and the *tantra,* of wine and women). They preached a simplistic religion with 'no *mantra* or *tantra'*. Called the *Sahajayani marga*, this trend, starting from the east, conquered the west up to Kabul and beyond. Goraknath, the greatest religious figure since Sankaracharya in the eighth century, was central to this enterprise. He was born in the tenth century. His followers, known as Nath-Panthi Yogis and, subsequently, Kabir and his Nirgun school of poets dominated the scene for 600 years till Ram and Krishna worship took over in the sixteenth century. This remarkable phenomenon of Nath-Panthi Yogis has passed out of our consciousness, though in north-western India, one could encounter them up to the nineteen-twenties. But its importance cannot be overemphasized.

The Turkic conquerors with their proselytizing creed, inevitably introduced a new element on the Indian scene. But in a fundamental sense the unity of Indian civilization was not disrupted. The conquerors, of course, spoke their own Turkish language in their homes and also Persian, which they had acquired in Afghanistan before coming to India, was the language of culture for them. But up to the second half of the sixteenth century Persian served only as the formal and official language at the court and of law courts administering the Shariat. It was then that, at Raja Todarmal's instance, it was made the language of the revenue department in place of Hindavi and other Indian languages. This gave Persian a new status since Hindu employees and aspirants to government jobs had to learn it. This was to culminate in the Persianization/Arabization of Hindavi to make it Urdu.

In the middle of the sixteenth century Malik
Muhammad Jayasi wrote his famous *Padmavati*, a work
of Sufi mysticism in the guise of a Rajput romance, in the
same language as Tulsidas wrote his *Ramacharitmanas*,
except that Jayasi used more of Prakritic elements than
Tulsidas who, as a Sanskrit scholar, leaned on that parent
language. It was in the Deccan, at the end of the century
that Persianized diction grew up in Dakhni Hindavi as a
result of the introduction of the Persian script. Members
of the Muslim ruling elite used the Hindavi they took with
them from the north to distinguish themselves from the
local Telugu- and Marathi-speaking people and they took
to the Persian script in assertion of their identity.

Professor Chatterjee writes: "Still, Deccan Hindustani
for two centuries did not cut itself off from ordinary Hindu
speech, and the vocabulary of king Muhammad Quli Qutb
Shah, the poet-king of Golconda (d.1611), and that of
other Sufi poets contemporaneous with and posterior to
him, had a good percentage of pure Hindi and Sanskrit
words. The Persianising writers of Delhi, Lucknow,
Lahore and Hyderabad-Deccan in the 18th and 19th
centuries worked a revolution in the spirit of Urdu, which
may as a result be properly described as the
Mohammedan form of Hindi." (See *Indo-Aryan and
Hindi*.)[19]

The foundations of two cultures and of partition had
thus been laid. Persianized Urdu was to play the role of
producing a rival cultural matrix which Persian itself
could not have done. But as it happened, the retreat of
Muslim power in the world as a whole and in India had
begun by then. Great Urdu poets came after the death
of Aurangzeb in 1707 and the beginning of the takeover
of India by the British East India Company after the
battle of Plassey in 1757. The great Ghalib was to seek
a stipend from the Company. This retreat was not to be
reversed. In India, as we shall see, it was to pave way

for the re-emergence of Hindus and Hindu civilization. This was, of course, not to be a revival which history does not permit. It was to be a return of the Hindu spirit in new forms, necessitated by the impact and dominance of the West, which still continue.

Hindu Nationalism: The First Phase

S ince the contribution of British Orientalists in the second half of the eighteenth century to the growth of self-awareness and pride in their past cultural achievements among educated Hindus is well known, it is rather surprising that the rise of Hindu nationalism should be traced back at best to the Arya Samaj in the late nineteenth century and, indeed, to the establishment of the Hindu Mahasabha and the Rashtriya Swayamsevak Sangh (RSS) in 1925 and 1926. Obviously, the record needs to be set straight and this perspective corrected.

The story begins in 1767 when John Zephaniah Holwell's pioneering work was published under the lengthy title *Interesting Historical Events, relating to the Provinces of Bengal and the Empire of Indostan.... As also the Mythology and Cosmogony, Fasts and Festivals of the Gentoos, followers of the Shastah, and a Dissertation on the Metempsychosis, commonly, though erroneously, called the Pythagorean doctrine.* Holwell's contribution to the European view of India was twofold: he established the great antiquity of the Indian people and the need to apply standards "other than European" to the study of India and its culture. Holwell dismissed previous accounts of India as "defective, fallacious and unsatisfactory...only tending to convey a very imperfect and injurious resemblance of a people, who from the earliest times have been an *ornament to the creation* if so much can with propriety be said of any known people on the earth".[1]

This story has been ably told, apart from O.P. Kejariwal, by P.J. Marshall in his *The British Discovery of Hinduism in the Eighteenth Century*[2] and David Kopf in his *British Orientalism and the Bengal Renaissance: The Dynamics of Indian Modernization 1773-1835.*[3] We do not need to go over that ground again except to make a couple of points.

It will be in order to quote here Sir William Jones's famous statement on Sanskrit because it helped restore Hindu self-confidence to a great extent, though it also gave birth to the Aryan race and Aryan invasion/migration theory which has not been disposed off till today despite the absence of any worthwhile evidence outside the uncertain discipline of philology. According to him:

> The Sanskrit language..., "whatever be its antiquity, is of a wonderful structure, more perfect than the Greek, more copious than the Latin, and more exquisitely refined than either, yet bearing to both of them a stronger affinity both in the roots of verbs and in the form of grammar, than could possibly have been produced by accident; so strong indeed, that no philologer could examine all three, without believing them to have sprung from some common source, which, perhaps no longer exists...there is a similar reason, though not quite so forcible, for supposing that both the Gothick and the Celtick, though blended with a very different idiom, had the same origin with the Sanskrit; and the old Persian might be added to the same family.[4]

That was not all. Jones also stressed the similarities between Vedanta and European philosophy. It was not possible for him, he said, "to read the Vedanta, or the many fine compositions in illustration of it, without believing that Pythagoras and Plato derived their sublime theories from the same fountain with the sages of India". Pieces of Sanskrit literature accessible to him, the six schools of Hindu philosophy and the laws of Manu, the religious myths and symbols and various cultural and architectural remains all testified for him to a "people with a fertile and inventive genius", who "in some early age...were splendid in arts and arms, happy in government; wise in legislation, and eminent in various knowledge...."[5]

The role of Sir William Jones as the father of comparative mythology is less well known among non-specialists. But it is equally significant. He compared the Gods of India, Greece and Italy. Thus, he found Janus similar to Ganesa; Saturn to Manu or Satyavrata; Jupiter to Indra; Hermes to Narada; and Ceres, daughter of Saturn, to Lakshmi. He also gave arguments to show that a group of Egyptian priests had settled down in India and borrowed much from it. He was certain that the connection between the two civilizations existed before Moses. This point has since been accepted, but not widely enough, and it also remains open to question whether Egypt communicated its knowledge of the arts and sciences to India, or vice versa.

Jones was followed by H.T. Colebrooke who specialized in the study of the Vedas. With his *Essay on the Vedas*, he established that the Vedic Hindus believed in the "unity of the godhead". The Jones-Colebrooke portrayal of the Vedic age "was the first reconstructed golden age of the Indian renaissance".[6] Its importance for the rehabilitation of Hindus in their own esteem cannot possibly be exaggerated.

Obviously, this "reconstructed golden age of Indian renaissance" could not have been sustained without a reconstruction of Indian history on the modern Western pattern. Again, Sir William Jones made the beginning. Only two clues were available to him — Alexander's invasion of India in 326 B.C. and the report of Megasthenes, Selecus Nicator's ambassador at an Indian emperor's court, which could be reconstructed, though the original had been lost. Megasthenes spoke of "Patlibothra" which he located at the junction of the Ganges and Erranaboas. Patlibothra could be identified with Patliputra, an earlier name of Patna. But what about Erranaboas which could not possibly be treated as a Greek distortion of the Son river? Sir Jones discovered a reference to Son as Hiranyabahu which rendered into Greek could become Erranaboas. Megasthenes had also spoken of Sandracottus. He could well be Chandragupta, but Chandragupta was not known then. Sir William found in an obscure political tragedy the story of Chandragupta the adventurer who ruled in Patliputra. Thus Indian history in modern form had been born.

The details of the foundation of Indian historiography have been well narrated, among others, by John Keay in his richly illustrated *India Discovered*[7] and need not detain us in this bird's eye view of developments in the last two centuries or so. Even so tribute must be paid to Warren Hastings who admired the Hindu inheritance and made its resurrection possible; James Princep, who deciphered the Brahmi script and thus facilitated the discovery of Emperor Ashoka, the most remarkable ruler in ancient India we know of so far; and Lord Curzon who ensured the preservation of India's great sculptural and architectural inheritance.

But for Curzon, this inheritance was in grave danger of being further depleted through sheer ignorance, indifference and vandalism. Curzon appeared on the Indian scene at the end of the nineteenth century. Much more could have been preserved if someone with a similar awareness had been India's governor-general in the first quarter of the century when the great monuments were discovered and identified. It speaks for the spirit animating the rulers of independent India that even roads named after Curzon and Hastings in New Delhi have been renamed.

As Kopf has put it: "The intellectual elite that clustered about Hastings after 1770 was classicist rather than 'progressive' in their historical outlook, cosmopolitan rather than nationalist in their view of other cultures, and rationalist rather than romantic in their quest for those 'constant and universal principles' that express the unity of human nature."[8]

Much of this was to change for the worse in the nineteenth century when nationalism and racism came to dominate the West European mind. The earliest expression of this change in our case is James Mill's *History of India* published in 1817. It was, in large part, written to refute the views of Sir William Jones. It marked the beginning of the triumph of the Anglicists (read detractors of India) over the Orientalists who were admirers of the Indian civilization. Thomas Macaulay clinched the issue in favour of the Anglicists with his famous minute in 1832. English was to become the medium of instruction and not Sanskrit and Persian which the Orientalists had favoured. In this new Anglicist discourse, India was misunderstood, misrepresented and run down in almost every conceivable way. This shameful history of the imperialist and hegemonic discourse has been discussed comprehensively for the first time by the American scholar, Ronald Inden, in *Imagining India.*[9]

This imperialist perversion in the name of knowledge made it out that Hindu society had got frozen just above the primitive level. In fact, studies of Africa served as the model for studies on India. This by itself is a fascinating story which has been narrated by Adam Kuper in *The*

Invention of Primitive Society.[10] The interesting point
about it is that this invention was, to begin with, the
handiwork of lawyers and not of anthropologists, who
moved into the act much later. It inevitably influenced
British civil servants and other Britishers and Europeans
who fed on it. It also undermined the development of the
Raj as a genuinely Indo-British enterprise. More
pertinently, it could not but distort the perspective of the
Indian intelligentsia which was to emerge as the
dominant force in the country as English became the
language of higher education, administration and justice.
The distortion produced alienation which, if anything, has
grown since independence for the obvious reason that the
countervailing power of nationalism and patriotism,
which the fact of imperialist domination brought into
existence, has weakened. The doctrine of socialism, and
of secularism, not as an expression of Hindu catholicity
but as an offshoot and ally of socialism, has played a
crucial role in this aggravation of alienation, which we
shall discuss at a later stage.

The Hindus were clearly not in a position to influence
the outcome of the struggle between the Anglicists and
the Orientalists. They would have had to accept whatever
the outcome. But even if that were not the case, they
would have faced the proverbial Hobson's choice. The use
of Sanskrit and Persian as languages of education would
have perpetuated the Hindu-Muslim cultural stalemate,
with the balance in favour of Muslims in view of the
existing status of Persian as the language of administration even in non-Muslim states such as those of the
Peshwas in Pune and of the Sikhs in Lahore. The
changeover to English tilted the balance in their favour,
but involved the risk of the continued subordination of
their culture and civilization to an alien one. This risk
could not be avoided and had to be lived with. And, of
course, Western education with English as the medium

of instruction, was not without its advantages. It, for instance, stimulated the development of Indian languages which appeared to have got frozen. The renaissance in Bengali language and literature can, for example, be directly traced to the publication of Nathaniel Halhed's *Grammar of the Bengali Language.*

By this reckoning, 1817, when the foundation of the Hindu College (now known as the Presidency College) was laid is another important date for the purpose of our narration. But whatever the date, the issue is the rise of the new intelligentsia which has been a crucial factor in the building of India today. But in addition to the Western impact, the point to emphasize is that this intelligentsia has not operated in a cultural-civilizational vacuum. India has not been a clean slate on which the British or the intelligentsia could write whatever they chose. Indeed, the slate has refused to be wiped clean. By way of illustration, it may be pointed out that Raja Rammohan Roy, justly regarded as the father of modern India by virtue of his leadership of the Brahmo Samaj, was no Westernizer in the normal sense of the term. For one thing, he met the challenge of Christian missionaries head-on and, for another, he made the Hindus suffering from loss of memory and pride aware that in the Upanishads they had an inexhaustible source of wisdom which no other civilization could claim to supersede. He justified the reforms that he campaigned for, such as the abolition of sati, in terms of ancient Hindu traditions and texts.

Keshub Chandra Sen provides a fascinating example of how the Hindus coped with the Christian and the Western challenge. He was a great admirer of Christ so much so that it was believed by, among others, Max Mueller that he was ready to be converted. And not without reason. For he said: "It is Christ who rules British India, and not the British Government. England has sent out a tremendous moral force in the life and character of that mighty prophet, to conquer and hold this vast empire. None but Jesus ever deserved this bright, this precious diadem, India, and Jesus shall have it."[11] Yet Keshub Chandra was strongly attracted and influenced by Ramakrishna Parmahansa, the teacher of Swami Vivekanand and the first of the great saints of the modern period who have helped shape the India we know.

David Kopf gives three reasons for this attraction which deserve attention. First, Ramakrishna was not susceptible to formal education, English or indigenous; this separated him from other Brahmos of whatever ideological bent. Secondly, Ramakrishna's Tantric way of sublimating the sensual drive for women into a spiritual drive for the Divine Mother appealed to Keshub Chandra. Third, Ramakrishna claimed to have experienced direct, intuitive contact with all major religious leaders in history. "In this sense, the Hindu Ramakrishna was perhaps more universalist and Brahmo than most of the Brahmo ascetics, who were narrowly Vaishnava." These three aspects of Ramakrishna's career as a mystic were probably strong influences on Keshub from March 1875 onwards, when the two men presumably first met at the Kali temple in Dakshineshwar. Keshub was intrigued by the religious "experiments" performed by Ramakrishna, and wished to adapt them to his own use, especially those elements of the Sakto tradition in Bengal that emphasized the "motherhood of God". (See David Kopf, *The Brahmo Samaj and the Shaping of the Modern Indian Mind.*)[12]

Kopf makes another significant point, which is notable not only because what he says about the Brahmos applied to most educated Hindus but also because it highlights another attempt at synthesis which is characteristic of Hindus. Most Brahmos, he says, viewed the Tantric tradition in Bengal as a debased form of religious expression, and a radical departure from the classical Hindu tradition. The idea of differentiating the good and bad features within Saktism, and incorporating the good into Brahmoism, probably came to Keshub after his acquaintance with Ramakrishna. For, in the early 1860s, Ramakrishna had already performed experiments to purify Saktism and Tantrism. "His experiments with religious behaviour dealt ultimately with the same problems of unity and diversity that had plagued Brahmos."[13]

In terms of dates, the importance of 1857 cannot be overstated. Whether one regards it as the first war of independence, as Veer Savarkar did, or the Sepoy Mutiny, as the British did, it is not open to question that its failure meant the emasculation of the old order and leadership, Hindu as well as Muslim, and with that, the closure of the era that opened with the arrival of Mahmud Ghaznavi in the eleventh century. The banishment of the last Mughal emperor, Bahadur Shah Zafar, symbolized the final eclipse of the old order just as imposition on him of the leadership of the uprising symbolized its continuing hold on the imagination of the people. It is not particularly relevant to discuss the nature of the old order, benevolent or malevolent, its character as a predominantly Muslim or a joint Hindu-Muslim enterprise in some periods and other similar questions in the case of a historical shift of this dimension. We are aware that in continuation of our pre-modern approach, most of us continue to discuss history in moral terms, but that only helps cloud our perspective, not clear it.

Inevitably, the emasculation of the traditional leadership had to pave the way for the rise to prominence of the new intelligentsia which had gradually grown in numbers and confidence since its small beginning in the early nineteenth century. As it happened, and not just by some accident, this intelligentsia was predominantly

Hindu in all three presidencies – Bengal, Madras and Bombay. As it also happened,this intelligentsia was ready, by virtue of the impact of Western political ideas, to take to the hitherto unfamiliar concept of nationalism even if with emphasis on the territorial aspect. The Indian National Congress established in 1885 was to be the vehicle of this class, to use this Marxist category for want of a better one. It is from here that the history of Hindu nationalism has to be traced and *not* from the dates of the establishment of the Hindu Mahasabha and the RSS.

Bankim Chandra Chatterjee synthesized the Western secular concept of nationalism with the tradition and needs of Hindus even if he was thinking in terms of Bengal and not India when he wrote his famous novel *Anandmath* which contained the patriotic poem *Bande Mataram* (hail to the Mother) that became the national anthem during the struggle for freedom. The very fact that this was replaced by Rabindranath Tagore's *Jana Gana Mana* after independence, as a concession to Muslim susceptibilities, highlights the nature of the freedom movement. Bankim Chatterjee gave us what Sri Aurobindo has described as the "religion of patriotism". Bankim described his own viewpoint not differently from Sri Aurobindo's. He wrote: "taking into consideration the condition of man, patriotism should be regarded as the highest religion."[14] This was the master idea of Bankim's writing. But this was not a mere intellectual idea. He embodied it in the Mother Goddess.

As Sri Aurobindo wrote in his work *Bankim-Tilak-Dayanand*: "Bankim...gave us the vision of our Mother.... It is not till the motherland reveals herself to the eye of the mind as something more than a stretch of earth or a mass of individuals, it is not till she takes shape as a great Divine and Maternal Power in a form of beauty that can dominate the mind and seize the heart that these petty fears and hopes vanish in an all-absorbing passion for our mother and her service, and the patriotism that works miracles and saves doomed nations is born."[15]

Bankim was not anti-Muslim. This point has been clinched by Arabinda Poddar.[16] In view of the importance of this question in a definition of Hindu nationalism, it would be in order to discuss his findings at some length. "*Anandmath*", he says, was "definitely and entirely an anti-British novel; the children of the Mother had little to do with Muslims, even when they were depicted as fighting against them." In the first edition of the novel, Bankim, while describing the battle in the third section, does not use the words "*yavan*" and "*nere*" (which implied Muslims), but in their place the word "*ingrej*" (the British) was consistently used. The substitution was clearly an afterthought intended to protect Bankim from the wrath of the British.

In the original edition of the novel *Sitaram*, the Fakir says: "Son, I hear that you have come to found a Hindu dominion; but if you be a slave to popular prejudices you will fail to achieve your aim. If you don't consider Hindus and Muslims as equals, then in this land inhabited by both Hindus and Muslims you will fail to keep your kingdom intact. Your projected Dharmarajya will degenerate into a realm of sin."[17]

Finally, in the epilogue to *Rajsinha*, Bankim writes, "...this novel was written not to differentiate between Hindus and Muslims.... In statesmanship Muslims undoubtedly were better than contemporary Hindus.... One who possesses, among other virtues, *dharma*, no matter if he be a Hindu or a Muslim, is the best...."[18]

Poddar cites reasons, specific to Bengal, as to why Muslims did not figure in Bankim's vision of the future. First, as occupants of the lower rungs of the caste hierarchy, "they simply did not count". But more important, Bankim was born a Hindu. "His intellectual quests, through a critical scrutiny of current European philosophies, reinforced his faith in Hinduism as the most rational and elaborate religion. If he sought to establish, in intellectual terms, the superiority of Hinduism to both Christianity and Islam, he thereby did not earn the right to be called a communalist."[19]

Swami Vivekanand represents the next phase in the development of the 'religion of patriotism'. Three points are notable in this regard – his identification of Mother India with the supreme God; his attempt to reintroduce the Kshatriya element in the Hindu psyche; and his conviction that India was destined to be teacher of the human race in the spiritual realm. On the first, he said:

> So give up being a slave. For the next fifty years this alone shall be our keynote – this our great Mother India. Let all other vain gods disappear for the time from our minds. This is the only God that is awake, our own race – everywhere his hands, everywhere his feet, everywhere his ears, he covers everything. All other gods are sleeping.[20]

On the second, he said:

> You will understand *Gita* better with your biceps.... What I want is muscles of iron and nerves of steel, inside which dwells a mind of the same material of which the thunderbolt is made. Strength, manhood, Kshatra-virya and Brahmateja.[21]

On his return to India after making a deep impact at the Parliament of Religions in Chicago in 1893, Vivekanand declared that the indebtedness of the universe to India knew no bounds. While civilizations had come and gone, the civilization of India was "indestructible and eternal". The message of this civilization had to be spread throughout the world. "For only Vedanta could triumphantly stand against the faith-killing, heartles rationalism of modern science; only Vedanta could lead men to salvation."[22]

Vivekanand believed that each nation, like each individual, "has one theme in its life, which is its centre, the principal note around which every other note comes to form the harmony. In one nation political power is its vitality, as in England, artistic life in another and so on. In India religious life forms the centre, the keynote of the whole music of national life".[23] There can be no question that Vivekanand represents a landmark in the rise of the Hindu people.

At the time of Keshub Chandra Sen and ahead of Swami Vivekanand, arose in north-western India a mighty force in Swami Dayanand and the Arya Samaj, which was to play a major role in awakening among the Hindus the spirit of self-confidence. This is a vast subject on which excellent studies exist. Here, we need not go into details of the Swami's life, teachings and activities. Some of the controversies which his teachings and activities provoked during his lifetime continue to reverberate. Those too do not belong here. We are concerned primarily with his place in the story of the re-emergence of the Hindu people. That place cannot be overstated. In Sri Aurobindo's words, it was a "master-glance of practical intuition" on his part "to go back trenchantly to the very root of Indian life and culture (the Veda), to derive from the flower of its first birth the seed for a radical new birth. And what an act of grandiose intellectual courage to lay hold on this scripture defaced by ignorant comment and oblivion of its spirit, degraded by misunderstanding to the level of an ancient document of barbarism, and to perceive in it its real worth as a scripture which conceals in itself the deep and energetic spirit of the forefathers who made this country and nation.... Rammohun Roy, that other great soul and puissant worker who laid his hand on

Bengal and shook her – to what mighty issues – out of her long, indolent sleep...stopped short at the Upanishads. Dayanand looked beyond and perceived that our true original seed was the Veda."[24]

There were similar movements in western India beginning with the Prarthana Samaj which threw up great social reformers such as Mahadev Govind Ranade and Gopal Krishna Gokhale. All in all, the foundations of Hindu nationhood had been firmly and widely laid. Out of these movements of re-formation in north-western India, western India and Bengal, emerged the triumvirate of Lal (Lala Lajpat Rai), Bal (Bal Gangadhar Tilak) and Pal (Bipin Chandra Pal) who dominated Indian politics in the first two decades of the twentieth century. Sri Aurobindo, then Arabinda Ghosh, joined them for a brief period at the time of the partition of Bengal. He then retired from political life to pursue the path of yoga and to illumine the path by his writings.

In this narrative, so far we have referred to the Indian National Congress only once tangentially. This has been deliberate because we have thought it necessary first to outline the parameters within which it would have to function if it was to be effective. More often than not, the cultural-civilizational framework has been sidestepped in discussions of the Congress. By and large, emphasis has been placed, in these discussions, on the one hand, on the growth of aspirations to equality with the British and unemployment among the educated intelligentsia, demands for Indianization of services and admission to exclusive British clubs and the impoverishment of India as a result of British policies, and, on the other, on the involvement or lack of involvement of Muslims in the Congress. This has produced a rather lopsided view of the freedom movement.

As is well known, in its formative phase, the Congress was dominated by moderate constitutionalists who believed in the bona fides of the British and practised the politics of petitioning the Queen, the British government and Parliament in London. The first big break in this kind of politics came with Lord Curzon's decision to partition the Bengal presidency in 1905. This provoked a fierce reaction among the Bengali *bhadralok* and produced the first mass movement since 1857. This was a turning point in modern India's political history. And it is hardly necessary to underscore the point that this was a Hindu movement even if it is true that some influential Muslims in Bengal were also opposed to partition.

Charles H. Heimsath provides us a good summing up in his *Indian Nationalism and Hindu Social Reform*.[25] He notes that up to the first decade of the twentieth century, the Indian National Congress had tried to define a new India in terms borrowed from "European political experience and western social ethics". But these ideals and methods had failed to win it much popular support. A "reconstructed Hindu nationalism", therefore emerged. Moderate constitutionalists like Dadabhai Naoroji, Gopal Krishna Gokhale, Pherozeshah Mehta and S.N. Banerjee were replaced by men such as Lajpat Rai, Tilak, Bipin Chandra Pal and Aurobindo, "all of whom identified the nation with the religious tradition of Hinduism".

As *Bande Mataram*, the extremist paper edited by Bipin Chandra Pal and Aurobindo Ghosh explained: "Swaraj as a sort of European ideal, political liberty for the sake of political self-assertion, will not awaken India. Swaraj as the fulfillment of the ancient life of India under modern conditions, the return of the *Satyayuga* (era of truth) of national greatness, the resumption by her of her great *role* of teacher and guide, self-liberation of the people for the final fulfillment of the Vedantic ideal in politics, this is the true Swaraj for India."

The paper further wrote, "the groundwork of what may well be called the composite culture of India is

undoubtedly Hindu. Though the present Indian
nationality is composed of many races, and the present
Indian culture of more than one world civilization, yet it
must be admitted that the Hindu forms its base and
centre.... The dominant note of Hindu culture, its sense
of the spiritual and universal, will, therefore, be the
peculiar feature of this composite Indian nationality....
And the type of spirituality that it seeks to develop is
essentially Hindu".

Similar sentiments were echoed by the Prarthana
Samajists of western India. Ranade declared in the 1880's
that there was little possibility of genuine reform unless
the "heart of the nation...is regenerated, not by cold
calculations of utility, but by the cleansing fire of a
religious revival". In North India the Arya Samaj leader
Lajpat Rai wrote: "In my opinion, the problem before us
is in the main a religious problem – religious not in the
sense of doctrines and dogmas – but religious in so far
as to evoke the highest devotion and the greatest sacrifice
from us." "The spiritual note of the present Nationalist
Movement in India," he said, "is entirely derived from...
Vedantic thought." In South India the Theosophical
Society leader, Annie Besant, proclaimed: "If there is to
be an Indian nation, Patriotism and Religion must join
hands in India."

As a result of this reconstructed Hindu nationalism,
"the demand for full independence was for the first time
understood by great numbers of Indians, and a sincere
pride in the Indian heritage made that demand into more
than an academic assertion of natural rights."[26]

As I see it, our history of the past two centuries has
been the history of the rise of Hindus after a lapse of
centuries of Muslim invasions and rule. This is a wholly

revisionist view of history and would be resisted by the dominant elite which has both made history in this period and written it. But precisely because mine is a radical departure, it merits being spelt out even if it is possible to do so only in bold strokes. I regard the task urgent in view of the havoc that history, as written and taught, has wrought.

The Hindu re-emergence took place under the auspices of the British, which is one reason why the phenomenon has not been seen to be what it has, in fact, been. The British disarmed the peasantry and established the rule of law; they ensured that education and commercial enterprise (and not the sword) would be the gateways to success and prosperity. These measures were a handicap for the Muslim elite which had all along relied on the sword to establish and sustain its hegemony.

The British, of course, had no desire to help in the re-emergence of Hindus. Indeed, after the formation of the Indian National Congress, they spared little effort to contain the rise of Hindus. The grant of separate electorates to Muslims and partition of the Bengal presidency, dominated by Western-educated Hindus in every field in 1905, were two such early steps. More were to follow, leading finally to partition in 1947. But even the mighty and shrewd British could not reverse the overall trend which they had promoted in no small way by undermining the Ottoman empire.

Broadly speaking, two processes have been on in Hindu society since the early nineteenth century — modernization based on the Western model and self-renewal through social reforms. The two processes have been interlinked and must be seen as such. In view of the obvious Western dominance in most fields of human activity, Hindus had no choice but to come to terms with it. Otherwise, they would have stagnated.

Muslim rule had debilitated Hindus to a point where a meaningful attempt at self-renewal was just not possible in the absence of the stimulus that the British provided. The degradation of almost one-sixth of the Hindu population to the status of untouchables, rigidity of the caste structure and excessive emphasis on rituals were expressions of that debilitation.

Hindus in sufficient numbers were ready to accept the British, as is evident from the demand for Western style education with English as the medium in Bengal. The Hindu College in Calcutta, it may be recalled, was established *before* the Anglicists won against the Orientalists and Macaulay wrote his famous minute. But the process of modernization would have been devastating in its consequences if it was not accompanied by a new awareness of, and pride in, our cultural heritage.[27] As it happened, British officials-scholars were busy discovering India's past. The discovery amply justified that pride.

This dual reality about Hindu society is not recognized sufficiently and widely enough in our public discourse. Thus it remains fashionable to speak of Raja Rammohan Roy as the 'father of modern India' and to ignore the contribution of Ramakrishna Parmahansa, though the latter and even more significantly, his disciple, Swami Vivekanand, helped restore self-respect and self-confidence among the Bengali *bhadralok* without which they could not have played the role they did in bringing about what is called the Bengal renaissance, precursor of a similar ferment in the rest of the country.

Similarly, it is a commonplace that the Indian National Congress was the handiwork of the Westernized intelligentsia and to disregard the point that it would have remained a body of petitioners if men such as Lokmanya Tilak and Mahatma Gandhi had not brought in the people with the help of ancient symbols and, indeed, if Swami Vivekanand had not paved the way for them. Thus while Tilak used external symbols such as the Ganesh festival, Gandhi made himself into an icon millions of Hindus virtually worshipped. All these three individuals can be said to have embodied in their persons the two processes at work in Hindu society.

This brings us to the question of the Mahatma's place in the story of the rise of Hindus. It is not easy to answer this question. I, for one, am ill-equipped to make the attempt since I cannot claim to have studied carefully what the Mahatma has spoken and written. But perhaps that is also an advantage in this kind of exercise.

For long I believed that faced with the interlinked problem of getting rid of British rule and reconciling Muslims to an independent India not under their own hegemony, Gandhiji subordinated the goal of Hindu self-reaffirmation to the goal of superficial Hindu-Muslim 'reconciliation'; superficial because it sought to avoid an honest discussion of the two faiths and civilizations and recognition of the reality that one of them must be in a position to define the broad framework for independent India if the existing stalemate and conflict were not to continue indefinitely into the future.

I was not certain whether Gandhiji had studied with enough care the history of Islam in India, especially of the so-called 'reform movements' in the eighteenth and nineteenth centuries seeking effectively to purge it of Hindu influences and practices and thus destroying the bridges connecting the two. I could find no explanation worthy of the Mahatma for his decision to accept leadership of the Khilafat movement. The decision, it seemed to me, revealed the great man's proverbial Achilles' heel.

On deeper reflection I am not so sure. It now seems to me Gandhiji put aside the issue of the pre-eminence of Hindu civilization because he was convinced that Hindus needed first to overcome their weakness. It is well known that when Mahatma Gandhi arrived on the Indian scene from South Africa, the effort to divide India on religious lines had taken hold and that he struggled all his life to undo the damage in vain. It is not equally well known that an effort to fragment Hindu society on linguistic and caste basis had also been on even much earlier and Gandhiji was able to contain it and instead build a powerful freedom movement. This aspect of the Mahatma's life has unfortunately got obscured with the result that not many of us are aware that Hindu consolidation on a political platform was a primary precondition for a successful independence struggle.

R.C. Zaehner in his work *Hinduism* has described Gandhiji's effort "as a struggle for the recovery of India's dignity, self-respect and soul".[28] This was the heart of the matter. India had to be independent in order to recover her dignity and self-respect. And it is indisputable that Gandhiji wanted to re-establish the integrity of Hindu society, to reactivate it, which is what the recovery of the soul would imply. This was a complex effort as it was bound to be. Gandhiji was not a revivalist; he could not have been as effective as he was if he had been just that. The sensibilities of modern educated Indians who constituted his battalions had changed too much as a result of the British impact and the reform movements mentioned earlier. So he reinterpreted the Gita to emphasize the primacy of *karma* (action) yoga for the purpose of legitimizing political activism. Though he professed to be a *sanatanist*, an orthodox Hindu, he was one of the greatest reformers Hinduism had seen. Like other reformers before him he sought solution to the problem of Hindu decline in social reform, with heavy emphasis on the removal of untouchability. As a result of his campaigns, for the first time in history, untouchables gained entry into temples.

Gandhiji was conscious that the old order had been too badly disrupted to be restored and that a new order had to be built, if India was again to become a coherent entity. That was primarily why Nehru came to play the critical role that he did in the country's life.

The differences between the Mahatma and Nehru, it needs to be emphasized, were less significant than the areas of agreement because Gandhiji accorded great importance to Harijan uplift and accommodation of Muslims in the economic-political order on terms acceptable to them. Surely no one can argue that any other Congress leader was better qualified to attend to these concerns than Nehru. Nehru was Gandhiji's legitimate ideological heir and his political status flowed from his ideological closeness to the Mahatma.

It is perhaps not sufficiently known that the Indian people have, since time immemorial, been preoccupied with the problem of founding their polity on *dharma*. Aristotle noted in his *Politics* on the testimony of a Greek historian (whose works are no longer traceable) that India was the only land where virtue was successfully made the basis of the political order. And the Mahabharat lists 16 *chakravartins* (universal rulers) who exemplified virtue. That doubtless ceased to be a reality long ago. But its memory continues to possess the Indian people.

Among the leaders of modern India, Gandhiji alone had the perspicacity to recognize that India's soul responds to embodiments of *dharma*. It was not merely good tactics that led him to give up the European dress for the sannayasi's loin cloth; he had an instinctive understanding of its appeal to the people. He was able to mobilize the Indian masses as no one else before or since precisely because he made himself into a Mahatma. Ordinary Hindus looked upon him as a saviour and educated Hindus found him irresistible. One has only to read an account of his one-day visit to Gorakhpur by

Shahid Amin in *Subaltern Studies*[29] to appreciate what
it meant to be Mahatma Gandhi. The people came to be
convinced that to be loyal to Gandhiji won them rewards
from heaven and to be opposed to him brought disasters
on them.

It was therefore not an accident that Gandhiji invoked
the mighty spirit of Lord Ram, whom the Hindus regard
as the seventh incarnation of Vishnu. For Ram of Balmiki
is no mere cultural hero as he has been made out to be.
He is, above all, an exemplar for the ordering of the
community's polity. That is why *shakti* (power) is regarded
as vital a component of his personality as *sheela* (conduct
suffused with a moral vision but not bound by traditional,
received wisdom).

Mahatma Gandhi could not have been thinking of
Ram only as a member of the Hindu pantheon when he
talked of Ramrajya. He was looking for an ideal concept
for the reordering of India's public life when it regained
the freedom to engage in such an effort. In that search
he landed, inevitably on Ram, inevitably because no one
else has ever better embodied the essence of Hinduism
in the public domain. Not even Yudhishtira; for his
pursuit of *dharma*, like those of his four brothers, was
one-dimensional uninformed as it was by a simultaneous
pursuit of *kama* and *artha* (pleasure and prosperity, in a
crude translation in the absence of exact equivalents).

Gandhiji's own life continued to be inspired and, in
fact, dominated, above all, by Ram. For him, as an
individual at the conscious level, politics remained an
extension of his religion, not in the narrow Semitic and
the equally narrow modern sense, but in the large Indian
sense which admits literally of millions of paths of self-
realization and of reaching God.

That is why Gandhiji sought Hindu-Muslim amity on
the platform of essential unity of the two 'religions' and
Nehru on that of a common fight against 'feudalism',

exploitation and poverty. Both approaches failed to produce the desired result; they had to fail. The two leaders tried to wish away the unresolved and stalemated civilizational conflict and they could not possibly succeed. The nobility of their purpose, the intensity of their conviction and the Herculean nature of their effort could not prevail against the logic of history. The alternative to partition would have been infinitely worse.

The importance of partition in 1947 for Hindus has been completely missed by the proponents of secular nationalism and Hindu *rashtra* alike. Though partition did not settle the civilizational contest that began with Muslim rule first in Sind and then in much of North India, it facilitated the task for Hindus since they now had a well-organized and powerful pan-Indian modern state of their own. As in the case of Europe, India could have remained a civilization and not become a nation. For it to be both, it needed the intervening agency of an effective pan-Indian modern state. The British provided us with such an agency. Regardless of whatever else they did, the importance of this contribution cannot be denied. On 15 August 1947, the Hindus finally became a *nation*, though not a *Hindu nation*. The distinction is important.

I have often said, half in jest and half in seriousness, that Muhammad Ali Jinnah was the greatest benefactor of Hindus in modern times, if he was not a Hindu in disguise. That has been my way of saying that partition was the best thing that could have happened for Hindus in the given situation in the mid-forties, because, without it, they could not have produced even a workable Constitution, not to speak of a viable economic and democratic political order. But it never occurred to me till recently that the Hindu-Muslim problem, as we faced it in the whole of this century, was the result of an old civilizational stalemate and that partition had finally ended it in favour of Hindus in three-fourths of India. I now believe that the civilizational unity of Hindus has been too pervasive and powerful to have been shattered by external onslaughts; that Islam in India has been too syncretistic and internally divided to be able to define itself in terms of its own values; that its apparent unity was largely the product of a deliberately fostered hostility to Hindus; and that nationalism in our case has to be pluralistic in its approach and has to centre on our civilization which is universal in the deepest sense of the term by virtue of its being the only primordial civilization to have survived intact and not to have degenerated into a narrowly defined religion. Indeed, it is precisely because Indian nationalism has been informed by a civilization remarkable for its catholicity and broadmindedness that it has not become a narrow creed. That is why it did not acquire an anti-Muslim bias either when the Muslim League unleashed widespread violence, as part of its campaign for Pakistan, or when Pakistan was, in fact, created.

To return to the subject under discussion, 15 August 1947 was a landmark in the rise of Hindus because we emerged as an independent civilization-nation-state. Hindu power was no longer open to challenge which it would have been in the absence of partition. But this reality could not be so defined not only because the Congress leadership was not trained to think in terms of civilizational contests but also because the shock of vivisection of Mother India was too great for most Hindus to allow them to realize that they had reached an important milestone on the road to recovery and reassertion.

The obvious connection between the stance of the leadership and the popular mood at the time of independence is not generally appreciated. This is rather surprising. After all, Nehru could not have survived for 17 long years in the office of prime minister with ease if the dominant sentiment among Hindus had not been generally favourable towards him and his broad policies. Independent India saw itself, and defined itself, in Western secular terms as a nation-state and not explicitly in civilizational terms as a Hindu *rashtra* for a variety of reasons. The Muslim factor was only one and not critically important to them at the deeper level of the Hindu psyche. At that level, Hindus have never seen any basic conflict between their heritage and Western science and technology and therefore the Western emphasis on rationality. The speed with which so many of them took to Western education and mores speaks for itself.

Till the eve of independence, Hindu thinkers emphasized the contrast between their spiritual heritage and Western materialism as part of the process of recovering their self-esteem. But in reality they needed to overcome the lopsidedness which an undue emphasis on piety at the cost of two of the central Hindu goals of *artha* and *kama* (prosperity and enjoyment) had produced in their lives in the period of their decline when they did not have a state of their own. They had to bury the *maya* (illusion) concept in its vulgar form in fact, if not the theory.

Retreat and Rage

The central issue that arises out of developments connected with the demolition of the Babri Masjid in Ayodhya on 6 December 1992 is whether the question relating to the civilizational base of the Indian state has finally been put firmly on the agenda, or whether it can again be put off, as it was after the First World War when Mahatma Gandhi took over the leadership of the nationalist movement from Lokmanya Tilak, who soon passed away. In the perspective of history, the answer has to be in the affirmative. The failure of the Marxist ideology in all its manifestations in practice, the collapse of most communist regimes all over the world and the disintegration of the Soviet Union itself have together created conditions in which Indian 'nationalism' can no longer be presented effectively in anti-colonial and civilization-neutral terms. Its civilizational base, structure and character cannot now be kept covered up for long by an ideological shroud. I am aware that a number of assumptions are implicit in these statements. These shall be substantiated as we proceed.

Before I take up this issue pertaining to the confusion of the true nature of Indian 'nationalism', however, it is necessary to correct the general perspective on the vital question of the role of Indian Muslims in the last two centuries which have witnessed the resurgence of India's ancient civilization in new forms appropriate to the spirit of our times. My perspective is different from that of proponents of Hindu-Muslim cultural synthesis or of composite Hindu-Muslim culture as well as that of advocates of undefined Hindutva.

This perspective is that Muslim power and therefore civilization have been on the retreat all over the world, including India, that this retreat has accounted for all movements we have witnessed in the Muslim world in the last two centuries, and that instead of helping check the retreat, these movements have promoted a ghetto psychology among Muslims. To put it differently, what has generally been regarded as Muslim aggressiveness and separatism, I treat as isolationism and opting out. I am in this essay, not concerned with the nature of Muslim conquest and rule.

To grasp the validity of this approach, it is necessary that we give up what may be called the 'frog-in-the-well' approach to history. Pandit Jawaharlal Nehru railed against this narrow approach but not to much avail. Indeed, in respect of the Hindu-Muslim civilizational encounter, he too suffered from the same handicap. Thus we discuss Mohammed bin Qasim's invasion of Sind in the eighth century more or less independently of the expansion of Arab Islam as far as North Africa and the Iberian peninsula in the west, with Mesopotamia, Syria, Egypt and Palestine thrown in, and Transoxania in the north, with the once mighty Iran, Medina, Khurasan and Sistan included in it. And more often than not we fail to take note of the fact that while Arab Muslim armies cut through Christian and Zoroastrian lands like knife through butter, in southern and eastern Afghanistan, the region of Zamindawar (land of justice-givers) and Kabul, the Arabs were effectively opposed for more than two centuries, from A.D. 643 to 870 by the indigenous rulers, the Zunbils and the related Kabulshahs. Though with Makran and Baluchistan and much of Sind, this area can be said to belong to a cultural and political frontier zone between India and Persia, in the period in question the Zunbils and their kinsmen, the Kabulshahs, ruled over a predominantly Indian rather than Persian realm. Arab geographers commonly speak of the king of *Al-Hind* "who bore the title of Zunbil". (*Zun* was a Shaivite God.) Andre Wink has detailed an equally prolonged resistance on the Makran coast in his *Al-Hind: The Making of the Indo-Islamic World*.[1]

Similarly, we discuss Babar's conquest of parts of North India without reference to the larger Turkish upsurge, culminating in the Ottoman empire, which, at its height, included present-day Albania, Greece, Bulgaria, Serbia, Romania, islands of eastern Mediterranean, parts of Hungary and Russia, Iraq, Syria, Palestine, the Caucasus, Egypt, north Africa (as far west as Algeria) and part of Arabia. This lopsided and parochial view of history was designed, perhaps deliberately, by British historians to inculcate in us a deep sense of inferiority. But whether deliberate or not, the effort succeeded remarkably well. Many educated Indians have accepted that everything worthwhile in India, including Sanskrit, has come from outside and that Indians have never been able to resist foreign invasions and occupations. Nirad Chaudhuri's *Continent of Circe* is perhaps the best-known expression of this British-promoted view of us as a degenerate people.

This gap between fact and history, as generally written and taught, is however, not my interest right now. I wish to emphasize that by the eighth century, Muslims had acquired from Spain to India "a core position from where they were able to link the two major economic units of the Mediterranean and the Indian Ocean....Muslims dominated all important maritime and caravan trade routes with the exception only of the northern trans-Eurasian silk route...the Arab caliphate from the eighth to the eleventh century achieved an unquestioned economic supremacy in the world...in monetary terms the result of the Muslim conquests was...a unified currency based on the gold *dinar* and the silver *dirham*.... Possession was taken of all important gold-producing and gold-collecting areas...."[2]

This economic supremacy provided so powerful an underpinning for the Muslim *ummah* (universal community of believers) and, therefore, civilization that they could survive all internal upheavals, including the Shia-Sunni divide; the decline of the Abbasid caliphate from the tenth century onwards, culminating in the sack of Baghdad in 1258 by the Mongols; the upsurge of Turks so much so that they can be said to have dominated the Islamic enterprise from the tenth century to the abolition of the caliphate in 1924. (The Safavid rulers of Iran too were Turkic and so were the Ghaznavids in Kabul.)

It follows not only that, to be fully effective, the challenge to Muslim dominance in that vast area had, in the final analysis, to be maritime but also that the *ummah* and Muslim civilization would find it difficult to survive in a meaningful sense the loss of control of the Mediterranean and the Indian Ocean. The Ottoman empire doubtless provided a second powerful underpinning. But its fate too was linked in no small way to the correlation of forces on the high seas.

Mediterranean Europe began to stir in the eleventh century. The crusades, beginning towards the end of the century, were an expression of that upsurge though they took a religious form. But the crusaders were first absorbed in the Muslim population and civilization and then beaten back. So, it was not before the end of the fifteenth century when Vasco da Gama discovered a new route to India via the Cape of Good Hope (out of Muslim control) and landed in India (in 1498), that a serious challenge to Muslim power can be said to have arisen. Though this challenge took around three centuries to mature and get consolidated, the impact on the fortunes of the Turkish empire was evident by the late sixteenth century, when the Dutch and the British were able to completely close the old international trade routes through the Middle East. As a result, the prosperity of the Arab provinces declined. The import of vast quantity of precious metals from the Americas following Spanish conquest and loot of that continent and the conversion of this gold and silver into currency also played havoc with the Turkish economy. Globalization of the world economy is, after all, not a twentieth century phenomenon!

This is a long and complicated story. The details, however significant and fascinating, like the retreat of the Turks from the gate of Vienna following defeat at the hands of the Hapsburgs in 1688, or Napoleon's invasion of Egypt in 1798, exactly three centuries after Vasco da Gama's voyage to India, need not detain us. What is material for our purpose is the steady erosion in Muslim control of the Mediterranean-Indian Ocean trade, the decline of the Ottoman empire and with that the replacement of the Islamic by the European civilization as the dominating reality on the world scene. The dismemberment of the Ottoman empire at the end of the First World War and the subsequent Turkish decision to abolish the caliphate in 1924 can be said to have completed the process. The two developments marked, in a fundamental sense, the closure of the era that opened with the establishment by the Prophet of the first Muslim state in Medina. However bitter and devastating the struggles within it and however painful the setbacks such as the sack of Baghdad in 1258 by the Mongols, the

ummah had been in control of its fortunes from
Mohammed's Medina period till then.

Since the beginning of the eighteenth century, Muslim
thinkers and men of action have tried to inaugurate a
new era in their history. Their failure to do so is obvious.
At various places, beginning with the seat of Ottoman
power in Anatolia itself, and at various times, beginning
possibly with Shah Waliullah in Delhi at the beginning
of the eighteenth century, they have tried different
strategies -- modernization of the armed forces and
administration, Western-style education, reinterpretation
of the Koran and return to pristine Islam, Western
ideologies from liberalism to Marxism via fascism, pan-
Islamism and pan-Arabism. Nothing has worked. (For
details see David Pryce-Jones, *The Closed Circle*.)[3]

The reasons for this world-wide failure are many and
complex. Among the most important is the nature of
Islam itself. Very early in its history, Islam closed itself
on itself. By insisting on the finality of Mohammed's
revelation and the immutability of both the Koran and
the Sunnah, Islam ensured that there could be no place
in it for self-renewal and there has been no self-renewal
in Islam as its students would accept.

To begin with there was a lot of free debate in Islam.
The presence of Mutazilites and Kharijites,[4] the rise of
major philosophers such as Ibn Sina and of Sufi orders
should help clinch the issue. As a result of Greek, Persian
and Indian influences and the consequent growth of
philosophy and sciences, early Islam, in fact, produced
and sustained an intelligentsia which, in the exercise of
free thought, took little account of the literal interpretation of the Koran. Sunni orthodoxy, though formul-
ated early in the Islamic enterprise, took centuries to
prevail. But once it did, in the thirteenth-fourteenth
centuries partly as a result of the work of Ibn Tamiyya,
it has reigned supreme.

Surprising though it may seem, the Western impact on Muslim societies has only strengthened the hold of orthodox Islam. In order to appreciate this point, it is necessary to recall that under the cover of a single terminology, two distinct religious styles have persisted among Muslims. As the well-known sociologist and Islamicist, Ernest Gellner, has put it: "Islam traditionally was divided into a 'high' form, – the urban-based, strict, unitarian, nomocratic, puritan and scripturalist Islam of the scholars; and a 'lower' form, the cult of the personality–addicted, ecstatic, ritualistic, questionably literate, unpuritanical and rustic Islam of the dervishes and the marabouts."[5]

It would be an exaggeration to suggest that the two traditions have always been at war with one another. For a variety of reasons, Sufi Islam has generally been at a disadvantage and has had to accommodate itself to orthodox Islam. Most Sufis, for instance, have acknowledged that the Shariat is immutable and binding on them as ordinary Muslims. Revivalist movements from time to time such as the Wahhabis have reinforced this disadvantage; Wahhabis fought bitterly against the saint cult which is the core of Sufi Islam. Even so, till recent times there had not existed a social base for a permanent victory of orthodox Islam over Sufi Islam.

Unlike earlier times, however, the colonial and the post-colonial states have been sufficiently strong to destroy the rural self-administration units or tribes that provided the base for the personalized, ecstatic, questionably orthodox, 'low' Islam and thus provided the base for a definitive, permanent victory of orthodox Islam over the other. This, Gellner argues, is the great reformation that has taken place in Islam in the last 100 years and in some ways made its hold on believers even stronger than before.

Neither the colonial nor the post-colonial state need have set out deliberately to weaken rural or tribal societies. That is the unavoidable logic of modernization by way of growth of large urban centres, the decline of rural communities and tribes in economic and political, if not in numerical, terms, and the spread of education, transportation and means of communication. Attempts to promote economic development, access to enormous resources by way of oil revenues, especially since the early seventies, remittances by emigrants to oil-rich Gulf states, and foreign aid were also bound to reinforce this logic.

The ascendancy of 'high' Islam also accounts for the failure of attempts at secularization in the Muslim world. As Gellner has put it, the presence of this genuinely indigenous tradition has helped Muslims escape the dilemma which has haunted many other Third World societies: the dilemma of whether to idealize and emulate the West or whether to idealize local folk traditions and indulge in some form of populism. They have had no need to do either because their own 'high' variant has had dignity in international terms.

Not everyone will agree with this assessment. Some Muslims have sought to emulate the West. Turkey, since the Tanzimat movement in the late nineteenth century, is one example and so is Egypt which was virtually an autonomous province of the Ottoman empire since about the same time. That these attempts failed is, in fact, a critical issue, but that cannot be dealt with here. Broadly speaking, the assessment is valid. Turkey and Egypt too continue to struggle to contain the tide of Muslim revivalism and fundamentalism.

There is another aspect of the Western impact which deserves attention. Millions of those who have been uprooted from the countryside and pushed into crowded slums and/or have found themselves left out of the benefits of modernization and economic development have sought and found solace in Islam. For them the language of Islam has become the means of coping with 'moral anxiety, social disequilibrium, cultural imbalance, ideological restlessness and problems of identity produced by the economic transformation of the post-independence period'.

The other major cause of the Muslim failure to move ahead is the *ummah* itself. In order to appreciate why this should be the case, it is necessary to know what the *ummah* is. This is particularly so because most non-Muslims, especially Hindus, have no idea what this community of believers means to Muslims and how it has managed to survive the rise and fall of dynasties in the past, endless intra-Muslim wars, the presence of around 50 independent Muslim states, the failure of pan-Islamism and other efforts to establish a coordinating centre.

To begin with, we should note, as Professor Francis Robinson has pointed out in his essay 'Islam and Muslim Separatism'[6] that the Muslim era does not begin with the birth of Mohammed, as the Christian era does with the birth of Christ, or with the first revelation of the Koran in Mecca, but with the *hijra* (migration) of the Prophet and Muslims to Yathrib (Medina) whereby the Muslim community was first constituted. This was to be no ordinary community. It was to be a charismatic community. That is why Mohammed could declare: "My community will never agree on error." That is why it was to function on the basis of *ijma* (consensus of the Muslim community or scholars as a basis for a legal decision) and suppress dissent. That is why this *ijma* was to play a critical role in the development and enforcement of the Shariat.

The well-known five pillars of Islam — bearing witness to the unity of Allah and finality of Mohammed's

Prophethood, prayers with special emphasis on collective prayers every Friday with the face always turned towards the Kaaba, *zakat* (charity) for purposes of the community, fasting during the month of Ramadan and Haj (pilgrimage) to Mecca – continuously reinforce this sense of the community. Much of this is familiar to all those who know anything about Islam. But Professor Robinson underscores a few points which deserve attention.

First, the last act of the Friday prayer itself commemorates the community as the Muslim turns to his neighbour on either side in performing the salaam. Secondly, no one who has lived with Muslims in the month of Ramadan can fail to see the powerful sense of community generated in the joint experience of fasting. Thirdly, the performance of the Haj represents the ultimate celebration of the community; for all pilgrims don two white sheets, the *ihram*, in recognition of the equality of all Muslims before Allah, and as they live for the first 13 days of the month on the plain of Arafat, they experience the reality of the community as never before despite differences of language and culture.

In addition, the use of the Arabic script has helped create Islamic languages out of non-Islamic ones, the transformation of Hindavi (or Hindi) into Urdu in India being a case in point. Similarly, Muslims use the same decorative patterns all over the world and segregate their women in the same way. Then there is the classical literature which has been carried wherever Muslims have gone and transmitted from one generation to another. This has produced a common cultural heritage which has defied being swamped by the most dramatic differences of environment, and of pre-Islamic cultures as, say, between India and Arabia. The Muslim personality is a reality despite regional and ethnic differences.

In view of the rise and fall of a number of Muslim dynasties, it is tempting to dismiss the *ummah* as a myth.

This temptation must be resisted. Despite the absence of central political control since the Abbasid caliphate, the *ummah* has been a potent reality and it remains so today. There has been no period in Muslim history when ideas and movements arising in one corner have not reverberated throughout the Muslim world. Non-Arab and non-Persian thinkers have written in Arabic and Persian precisely because they have seen themselves as part of the larger Islamic community of which these have been the languages of discourse and because they have sought influence throughout the Muslim world. Iqbal, for instance, wrote much of his poetry in Persian in British India in this century, though Persian had long ceased to be the language of discourse in this country. As for ideas and movements, if the Wahhabi influence emanating from Mecca dominated the Muslim mind in much of the nineteenth century, Maulana al-Mawdidi in this century can be said to have fathered what is now called 'Islamic fundamentalism'.

Trouble arises because while the *ummah* cannot throw up and sustain a directing or even a coordinating centre, it robs different groupings of the right to manage their affairs as independent political entities. That so ancient a people as the Egyptians should have abolished the very name of their country at one stage speaks for itself. Egypt continued to be called the United Arab Republic even after the union with Syria arranged in 1958 had been dissolved in 1960. Equally significant, it went to war with Israel in 1967 and invited disaster upon itself for a cause – Palestine – which was not specifically Egyptian. Today, Iranians are ready to put their future at risk in search of leadership of the *ummah*, because the Islamic revolution derives its legitimacy from that search. We can hear echoes of the Kremlin-Comintern debate in the Islamic vocabulary in Tehran. Turkey, on the other hand, can be said to have opted for an independent destiny since the abolition of the caliphate in 1924. In its case, the pull of Europe may prove stronger than that of Islam. But such an outcome is by no means assured in view of the rising appeal of political or radical Islam there too. The hitherto dominant pan-Turkish sentiment has also begun to stir as a result of the rise of independent Muslim states in Central Asia in the wake of the disintegration of the Soviet Union.

It is a commonplace that the *ummah* cannot have and does not have a fatherland or motherland. What is not equally well known is that this is as much the result of the persistence of tribalism as of universalism in Islam. Its remarkable military victories first under the leadership of Arabs and then of Turks at once helped validate its universalism and preserve the earlier tribalism of Arabs as well as of Turks. A tribal society is by definition a closed order; disputes among tribes tend to be a zero-sum game in view of the acute scarcity of resources; resort to violence is natural and normal in such circumstances; the outsider cannot be trusted. This face of Islam does not attract the attention the other universalist one does. But it is equally important. The implications are horrendous for Muslims: political communities cannot crystallize and get consolidated; governments continue to be dominated by tribal and clannish considerations; rule of law and democratic governments remain out of the question. *The Closed Circle* provides frightening details.

By its nature, the *ummah* has to be conservative. It had no choice but to close the door of *ijma* (consensus) as soon the judicial structure had been put in place by the four schools – the Shafi, the Maliki, the Hanafi and the Hanbali. All subsequent attempts to permit *ijtihad*[7] had to fail, especially in the absence of caliphal power which could offset the hold of the ulema. Political power can maintain a measure of equilibrium *vis-à-vis* the ulema. But there are limits to it as well, as Pakistanis have discovered. For dictators and populist leaders too find it not only useful but also necessary to appeal to the Islamic sentiment which remains pretty strong.

The *ummah*'s hankering after a saviour flows from its character and so does the commitment to return to pristine Islam or the golden age of Islam – the Medina period of the Prophet and the first four 'rightly guided' caliphs, three of whom, incidentally, were murdered. Though a Shia and an Iranian, Muslims were ready to hail Ayatollah Khomeini as Mahdi. The war with Iraq cut him down to size. Saddam Hussain would have been a Muslim hero if he had followed the invasion of Kuwait with that of Saudi Arabia and thereby blocked a Western riposte. He is again trying to recapture the imagination of fellow Muslims by his defiance of the US and the UN and he may well succeed.

In the nature of things, it was only to be expected that fundamentalist groups would arise in several Muslim lands. Whatever its rationale in terms of corrupt and tyrannical rulers and betrayed hopes, this upsurge is an exercise in self-destruction, though others cannot escape the fallout if only because two-thirds of the world's proven oil resources are locked in the Gulf region. All in all, Islam as a civilization is at bay. It is not encircled; it is closed from within. It cannot escape from the closed circle.

We have noted that just as control of the Mediterranean-Indian Ocean trade accounted for the success of the Islamic enterprise from the eighth to the sixteenth century, despite endless wars and rise and fall of dynasties, its loss by the end of the sixteenth century gravely weakened the Ottoman empire, the sword and shield of Islam in its encounter with the rising power of the West. The same factor was to play a critical role in the rise of revivalist movements beginning with the eighteenth century. The implication should be obvious, though it is seldom drawn, especially by Muslim scholars. The revivalist movements too represent the retreat of Islam.

The history of Muslim revivalism cannot be gone into meaningfully here. It will suffice to draw a distinction between Islamic *revivalism* and *fundamentalism*. The two are *not* interchangeable synonyms, though they are often so treated. They are too very distinct phenomena, belonging to two different periods in history. Revivalism followed the beginning of the decline of the three great Muslim empires – Ottoman in Turkey, Safavid in Iran and the Mughal in India. Political and economic factors had a great deal to do with the decline, though consensus emerged in each case that it was the result of a lapse on the part of Muslims from true Islam and that it could be reversed if Muslims were to return to it.

As Yousef M. Choueiri puts it in *Islamic Fundamentalism*: "Islamic revivalism was a reaction against the gradual contraction of internal and external trade, brought about by the mercantile activities of European nations.... Slaves, gold, spices, tea and textiles were the major bone of contention between various central Islamic governments and the seaborne empires of Europe."[8]

With reference to the rise of the Wahhabi movement, which has doubtless deeply influenced the course of Muslim history, Choueiri adds: "More importantly, the dominant position of the British in Indian textiles, spices and indigo diverted the Gujarat-Red Sea trade route away from Arabia. The British ascendancy precipitated the commercial collapse of the foremost Arabian ruler, the Sharif of Mecca. He consequently lost his ability to act as patron of various tribes or to continue to employ those of Central Asia in his trading activities. Wahhabism managed to rally under its banner tribes which were most adversely affected by this turn of fortune."[9]

Choueiri lists other similar movements resulting from European economic penetration – the Padri movement in

Sumatra between 1803 and 1837; the Faraizis in Bengal from 1820 to 1860; the Sunusiyyas in the tribal region between the Mediterranean coast and Chadian territories; and those in Sudan and Somalia. Though not always, as in the Indian case, the revivalist centres of action were often geographical peripheries of areas lying outside the control of central authorities, their social composition consisting mainly of tribal confederacies or alliances organized into new orders.

As such, revivalist movements from Sumatra in the east to Nigeria in the west in the eighteenth and nineteenth centuries conducted a purely internal dialogue, centred on the tenets and prescriptions of early Islam. "Thus, there was no reference to other systems of thought, either for comparative purposes or in order to introduce new elements, and no recognition of the superiority of other cultures was contemplated."

There was another Muslim response to the West in the ascendant – the reformist response which can be said to have begun with the Tanzimat movement in Turkey at the turn of the century and ended in 1967 with the defeat of Egypt under the leadership of President Abdel Nasser. Nasser, as is well known, had forged the pan-Arab sentiment into a powerful movement which, despite its Islamic trappings, did not look to the supposed golden age of Islam and instead sought to relate itself to the present via close relations with the Soviet Union and other communist countries, and via industrial growth through planning and basic industries in the public sector. The movement was flawed from the start. Pan-Arabism denied the legitimacy of territorial states and introduced an element of adventurism into Egypt's policies. It was too dependent for its legitimacy on hostility to Israel. Planning and heavy investment in public sector enterprises spawned a regime of corruption and failed to produce adequate returns. Even so, it represented a continuation of the reformist impulse. Its failure left the field open to Islamic fundamentalism.

Under Islamic reformism, Islam was for the first time dissected and re-evaluated; Western norms and concepts were borrowed; and the self-sufficiency of Islam was shattered. Liberty, constitutionalism and public interest came to be regarded as the key to progress and material achievement. The concept of *shura* (consultation), provided for in the Koran, was rediscovered and interpreted to imply parliamentary democracy. *Ijma* (consensus among the ulema) was similarly equated with public opinion. The well-known advocate of pan-Islamism, Jamal al-Din al-Afghani, belonged to the group of reformers as much as Sir Sayyid Ahmed Khan in India and Muhammad Abduh in Egypt. Al-Afghani, in fact, sought to demolish the edifice of Islamic philosophy by pointing out its anachronism and futility in the age of modern science and technology.

The reformist phase has to be broken up into two — the period of the ascendancy of Western style liberals and that of military officers and others who sought inspiration first from Nazism and fascism and then from communism. The second period followed the failure of the liberals.

The causes for the failure of liberal reformism should be obvious to students of Islam. The reinterpretation of key concepts like *shura*, *ijma* and *ijtihad* involved an attempt to ignore the history of Islam. It was an exercise in make-believe which could never succeed. The principle of liberty cannot possibly be reconciled to the reality of the *ummah* and the belief in the Koran being the immutable word of God to be taken in the literal sense; *shura* (consultation) was a pre-Islamic tribal institution which has not figured in Muslim history which has throughout been dominated by despotic rulers; the alternative has been anarchy, for such is the structure of Muslim society.

Indeed, that has been the rationale for the dominant ulema view that the worst kind of ruler is better than none. Thus when fascism and Nazism rose in Europe in the wake of the First World War, liberalism quickly lost ground in West Asia. This is a long story which is not material to the present discussion. The pertinent point for us to note is that this trend culminated in military takeovers in Egypt, Syria, Iraq, Indonesia and Algeria in the post-war period. With the exception of Indonesia, these regimes sought inspiration from the Soviet Union and communist China, which had replaced Nazi Germany and militarist Japan as the powerful opponents of the West. They too failed to deliver and it is this failure that has facilitated the rise and spread of fundamentalism.

Between 1856 and 1950, Muslim scholars attached to Islam all the labels available to them from the West — rationalism, science, nationalism, democracy and finally socialism. After 1970, the fundamentalists have come to reject all that. Unlike the revivalists and the reformers, they are not concerned primarily with rescuing Muslims from stagnation and ossification. They are possessed by the passion to reinstate Islam as the bedrock of the *ummah* in opposition to Western concepts and values, nationalism being one of them. In that sense, it is a contemporary reaction to 'revolutionary' nationalism and relatively secular forms of government as sought to be practised in several Arab lands under the banner of Arab nationalism.

Up to the 1970s, fundamentalism was more of an intellectual current than a serious political movement. Maulana al-Mawdidi is rightly regarded as the initiator of this current. The Iranian revolution in 1979 marked the first major success of the movement. This has been followed by the fundamentalist takeover in Sudan with the help of the army. But it is their sweeping victory at the polls in Algeria in December 1991 that sent warning bells ringing, loud and clear, in the dominant Western world which determines what the rest of us think and do.

Growing support for Islamic fundamentalism completes the era which began with the Prophet's *hijra* (flight) to Yathrib (Medina) and the establishment of the *ummah*, on the one hand, and the retreat of Islamic power, as represented by the Ottoman empire, that began towards the end of the sixteenth century, on the other. Iran is seeking to reverse this retreat and inaugurate a new era.

This dual significance of the Islamic revolution in Iran has been missed for a variety of reasons. To begin with, it was dismissed as a Shia affair made possible by the tradition of martyrdom in Shiaism, as illustrated by self-flagellation in the observance of Moharram, and the autonomy the Shia clergy in Iran, unlike the Sunni ulema, has traditionally enjoyed, *vis-à-vis* the state. Then it was obscured by the war with Iraq, which, to an extent, took the form of the age-old Iranian-Arab conflict. Even when the war was finally over in 1988, no attention was paid to the pre-eminent position Iran had in the meantime acquired in Sudan, which had been converted into a champion of Islamic fundamentalism.

Thus, it was only when Sudan's role, with Tehran's backing in the training of Algerian and Egyptian fundamentalists in particular came to be highlighted in 1991 that Iran's potentiality came to be properly appreciated. Indeed, judging by the media, the spotlight turned on Iran finally in 1992 when it made massive purchases of state-of-the-art weapon systems from Russia and reports began to circulate that it was trying to acquire nuclear weapons and missile capability with the support of China.

Clearly, it is premature to assess Iranian prospects. But two general points can be made. First, fundamentalism is inherently incapable of stimulating and releasing creative energies which can mark the beginning of a renaissance in Iran and the rest of the Muslim world. Secondly, fundamentalism can generate enormous fervour and energy. While it is open to question whether or not it can be channelized, its destructive potential is obvious.

Again, it is too early to say whether Islamic fundamentalism is likely to move up on the West's agenda. In the wake of the collapse of the Soviet Union, however, Westerners are more willing to face this reality than they were before. Indeed, earlier they regarded Islamic fundamentalism as an ally against communism. Witness the US support for the fundamentalists among the Afghan Mujahideen till as late as 1991.

Be that as it may, however, we are probably witnessing a shift in Western policy orientation similar to the one at the end of the war against Nazi Germany in 1945, when the Soviet ally suddenly got converted into a mortal foe. By way of illustration, we may refer to Brian Beedham's article: 'Turkey Star of Islam'.[10] He wrote: "The appropriately crescent-shaped piece of territory that starts in the steppes of Kazakhstan and curves south and west through the Gulf and Suez to the north coast of Africa [is] notably liable to produce turmoil and mayhem on a large scale in the coming 15-20 years."

Not counting non-Muslim Israel, the area does not yet have a single working democracy. "Worse, it does have an ideology. Now that Marxism has been lowered into its grave, Islam is the 20th century's last surviving example of an idea that claims universal relevance.... Not all Muslims are ideologues; probably most are not. Enough are to make Islam an uncomfortable neighbour."

Barry Buzan dwelt on the same ideological theme in 'New Patterns of Global Security in the 21st Century': "The collapse of communism as the leading anti-Western ideology seems to propel Islam into this role...and many exponents of Islam will embrace this task with relish. The anti-Western credentials of Islam are well established and speak to a large and mobilised political constituency."[11]

In an article entitled 'Defending Western Culture', that was written before the collapse of the Soviet Union, William Lind drew attention to another aspect of the threat to the West: "If the Soviet Union dissolves, the West's great right flank, stretching from the Black Sea to Vladivostok, will almost certainly be endangered as the Islamic republics seek to join their Muslim brethren."[12]

Western analysts are, of course, not insensitive to the fact that Islamic fundamentalism is, in no small measure, a reaction against utterly corrupt and inefficient regimes which have sought to keep themselves in power through slogan-mongering and ruthless suppression of even vague suspicions of dissent. But the emphasis is beginning to shift to the inherent incompatibility between Western values such as democracy and plurality and Islamic fundamentalism with its accent on the Koran and the Hadith as the sole sources of not only morality but also legality.

The emphasis appears, on the face of it, to be misplaced, in view of the fierceness of the Muslim world's own all-too-numerous conflicts and rivalries. But fundamental changes have taken place in Islam as such, ironically, largely as a result of the Western impact, which give it a long-term militancy and capacity to confront the West, though in the role of a disrupter and not that of an architect of a rival world order. This incidentally was also all that the communists were capable of under the leadership of the Soviet Union.

The point that developments in Indian Islam must be viewed in the larger context of world Islam cannot be overemphasized. For central to Muslims in India, as

anywhere else, is the *ummah*, the universal community
of believers. This does not mean that Indian Muslims
have been at the receiving end in this world-wide interaction of Islamic thought and practice. On the contrary,
Indian Muslim theologians have, from time to time, made
valuable contributions to the *ummah*. It is not for nothing
that one of the best known Arab historians, Albert
Hourani, has described the eighteenth century as the
century of Indian Islam.

This membership of the larger *ummah* does not also
mean that there has been nothing specifically Indian
about Indian Islam. It would have been surprising if this
had been the case.[13] But when we talk in civilizational
terms which is necessary in view of the universal nature
of Islam, issues have to be framed in the broader context.

It seems to me incontestable that, as in the larger
Islamic world, Muslims have been on the retreat in India
also. While the process of Hindu self-renewal and self-
affirmation has been on since the latter part of the
eighteenth century no similar process has been in
evidence among Indian Muslims since the battle of
Plassey in 1757. Indeed since the decline of the Mughal
empire, beginning with Aurangzeb's death in 1707, the
first priority of Indian Muslims, albeit not quite conscious
and well-articulated, has been self-definition and self-
preservation and not self-advancement. All major movements among them, beginning with Shah Waliullah[14] in
the eighteenth century, have been inspired principally by
this concern for demarcation from Hindus and Hindu
practices which the converts had brought with them.[15]

On a surface view, the Muslim League's campaign for
a separate homeland, culminating in the state of Pakistan
in 1947, cannot be clubbed with movements of demarcation and definition such as the Faraizi, Wahhabi,
Tablighi and so on. Indeed, the memory of having been
India's rulers figured prominently in the mental makeup

of the leaders and supporters of the Pakistan movement. Even so, the fear of being swallowed back into the Hindu 'ocean' gave it the sweep and power that it acquired even among Muslims who were to stay on in the Indian republic. Political separatism was an offshoot of religious separatism.

Professor Yogendra Singh in *Modernization of Indian Tradition*[16] has compared and contrasted Sanskritization among Hindus with Islamization among Muslims. Both are forms of upward mobility whereby lower sections of society seek to improve their status. But there the comparison ends. Professor Singh notes two differences. First, while "revolt against hierarchy through Sanskritization implies a withdrawal from tradition...and might eventually accelerate the pace of modernization", Islamization, "as a movement of revivalism of basic virtues in the Islamic tradition...might contribute to greater conservatism by increasing the hold of the religious elites on the population."[17]

Secondly, he writes, "the movement of Sanskritization is in no way approved by Brahmin priests and yet it goes on. Islamization, on the contrary, is not only engineered by the religious elites but results into [sic] an enhancement of their hold on the Muslim masses. It is thus a traditionalizing movement *par excellence*."[18]

Seen in this perspective, two interrelated propositions become obvious. First, the determined bids by Faraizis, Wahhabis, Al-Hadithis and Tablighis to remove Hindu influences and practices from the lives of ordinary Muslims and to block Western ideas and ideals were part of one single movement and, as such, one programme could not be separated from the other. Secondly, the presence of Hindu elements in Indian Islam alone could make its modernization possible by way of exposure to, and acceptance of, Western values; their elimination inevitably closed Indian Islam to modernization. But for the British tilt towards them, necessitated by the compulsions of the Raj, Indian Muslims would have faced marginalization long before 1947.

I would like to discuss here Sir Sayyid Ahmed Khan's role in the modernization of Islam and therefore in checking the general retreat of Islamic civilization. Sir Sayyid was greatly influenced by the Naqshbandi order, Shah Waliullah (the eighteenth century reformer) and Sayyid Ahmed Barelvi,[19] the Wahhabi leader who revived the principle and practice of *hijra* (migration from *dar-ul-harb*, land of war or those lands not under Muslim rule, where, under certain circumstances war can be sanctioned against unbelievers) and *jihad* (holy war against non-Muslims). Sir Sayyid saw the world as a Muslim, as Professor Francis Robinson puts it.

This does not mean that Sir Sayyid's attempt to interpret the Koran in terms of laws of nature, or Western learning, did not involve innovation. It did. If men such as Jamaluddin Afghani, the leading pan-Islamist of the nineteenth century, ridiculed him as a *nechari* (naturist – his efforts to harmonize the laws of Islam with nature earned him this title), they were justified. But his own intention was to strengthen the appeal of Islam, to "reveal to people the original bright face of Islam", as he put it, and make it possible for young Muslims to imbibe Western learning and yet remain Muslim.

His intentions apart, however, Sir Sayyid did not have the capacity to impose his view of compatibility between the Koranic revelation and miracles, on the one hand, and modern science, on the other, on the Muhammadan Anglo-Oriental College which developed into the Aligarh Muslim University. The whole enterprise would have ended in smoke if he had not surrendered control of theological education at Aligarh to Ali Baksh, one of his bitterest critics on that issue.

So fierce was the opposition that Sir Sayyid had to agree not to have anything to do with students in order to pacify his critics. Of his two successors, it may be noted that Viqar al-Mulk was profoundly interested in increasing the Islamic content of education and daily life at Aligarh and Mohsin al-Mulk played a leading role in the politics of the Muslim League.

This brings me to Aligarh's central role as an instrument of Muslim separatism. It produced young men deeply conscious of being Muslims and capable of operating effectively in the modern world, which the ulema, by and large, were not. While the latter could provide support to modern political movements, as they in fact did to the Khilafat movement and the Muslim League's campaign for a separate homeland, they could not promote and lead such movements. The leadership of the Khilafat movement, it may be recalled, centred on Muhammad Ali and Shaukat Ali, both products of Aligarh and not on Maulana Abul Kalam Azad. Aligarh students served as the League's storm troopers.

It has long been accepted that the cause of education among Muslims in the then North-West Province would not have suffered if the Aligarh University had not been established. Muslim presence in educational institutions in Bengal was abysmally low. In the North-West Province, if anything, it was in excess of the size of the Muslim population. Aligarh only gave education a Muslim and, therefore, separatist dimension.

Sir Sayyid himself was not a separatist for much of his life though he became one in the last phase. But that issue is not under discussion here. What is important is that Sir Sayyid proved a failure as a modernizer. Instead, his efforts to promote Western education among Indian Muslims produced an explosive mix of 'nationalism' and Islamic revivalism, of which partition of India in 1947 was only the first disastrous result. For Pakistan has yet to

learn to cope with it. Islamic fundamentalism is making
it extremely difficult for Pakistan to function as a normal
nation-state. In ideological terms, fundamentalists dominate
the scene; only ethnicity is able to offer some kind of
resistance to them.

The second observation I wish to make in the
discussion on Indian Islam follows from the first. It seems
to me that Indian Muslims view themselves, above all
else, as a religious community and a threat to that status,
real or imaginary, is what moves them deeply. By that
reckoning I do not see Indian Muslims as a political
community in being or in becoming. This assessment is
contrary to much that has been written on the subject
for a long time, especially since independence which is at
once surprising and unsurprising. Surprising because the
survival of pre-1947 responses and formulations speaks
of an incapacity to take into account so significant a
development as the elimination, on the one hand, of a
powerful agency (the British Raj) which could manipulate
the forces at play in the country and, on the other, of the
western Uttar Pradesh-centred Muslim elite which could
make common cause with that agency. Not unsurprising,
partly because events leading to, and following, partition
could not but have a traumatic impact on us and partly
because partition violated the very concept of territorial
nationalism which in the secular realm has served as
India's main *raison d'être*.

Muslim separatism, as it developed in British India,
has been discussed extensively and competently. Even so,
it is necessary to make some points in order to be able to
discuss post-1947 developments in a meaningful way.

First, the British Raj in India was critically dependent
on collaborators; it just could not have survived otherwise.
The collaborators came from both the old and the new
(British-produced) order. If Sir Sayyid Ahmed Khan chose

the path of collaboration, so did most leading Hindus of that period. His Persian ancestry is relevant in this context. He spoke for the Persianized Muslim elite centred in western UP which played a crucial role in the rise of Muslim 'nationalism', leading to the formation of Pakistan. There is no similar Persianized Muslim elite in today's India and there is no power with which such an elite, even if it had somehow survived partition and subsequent modernization, could have combined. Second, even the first step towards Muslim 'nationalism' could not have been taken in British India in the absence of separate electorates. This British move did not prove decisive, as the poor performance of the Muslim League in the elections to the state legislatures in 1937 showed; in the Muslim-majority provinces of Bengal and Punjab, the dominant Muslim parties and leaders made common cause with the relevant sections of Hindus — the poor and the landless in Bengal and the Hindu and Sikh land-owning peasantry in Punjab. Even so, separate electorates laid the basis of Muslim separatism. Our founding fathers abolished separate electorates and, mercifully for us, our rulers have not yielded to the pressure for allowing the dangerous scheme to make a re-entry by the back door, which is what the demand for proportional representation amounts to.

Even joint electorates could have left some space for a Muslim political community if there were a sufficiently large number of Muslim-majority constituencies in independent India. But outside Jammu and Kashmir, there are only two such parliamentary constituencies in the whole of the Union of India.

Muslim 'nationalism' found its 'fulfilment' in the formation of Pakistan if anything so artificial (it was all along propped up by the Raj) and so negative (it arose out of the fear of Hindu domination in free India) could find 'fulfilment'. Inevitably that 'fulfilment' marked its demise not only in India, where the necessary conditions for its rise and growth inevitably disappeared but also in Pakistan. For Pakistan has been an utter failure in terms of the ideology of Muslim 'nationalism'.

Within a couple of years of the establishment of Pakistan, the Punjabi identity asserted itself over Islamic universalism, provoking the assertion of language-based Bangla cultural identity which culminated in a sovereign Bangladesh in 1971.[20] Incidentally, this was the first case of a country breaking up under the weight of its own contradictions after the Second World War.

And what has remained of Pakistan since voluntarily serves the ends of the United States which must, by the very logic of its being, seek to undermine any Islamic assertion anywhere. Finally, the intensity of intra-ethnic clashes in Karachi and elsewhere speaks for itself. Pakistan is a grand failure in terms of its self-definition and the Indian Muslims know it in the heart of their collective heart even if they do not wish to take note of the total disarray in Muslim West Asia, including the Gulf region.

Seen in rational terms from the perspective of Indian Muslims, partition was one of the greatest tragedies in the history of Islam in India. They felt orphaned as they felt orphaned after 1857. And they returned to the collaborationist role that Sir Sayyid had recommended to them after 1857 – this time with the Congress government. Nehru made it relatively easy for them to do so by ignoring their role in the country's partition and by denouncing as more dangerous the 'majority communalism' (his expression) which existed largely in his own imagination. But I for one doubt whether the Muslim response to the new situation would have been very different if Nehru's pronouncements had been closer to the reality on the ground which was that the Hindus did not constitute a community in any relevant sense of the term, or if someone else was India's first prime minister, provided, of course, that he fulfilled his obligation of ensuring that the Indian Muslims could enjoy their rights as Indian citizens.

By virtue of its commitment to territorial nationalism which, unlike ethnic nationalism, does not exclude any group from full citizenship, and secularism and democracy based on adult franchise which emphasize the same principles of non-discrimination and equality, independent India at its birth was very different from British India in the nineteenth century. It offered Indian Muslims a unique opportunity to share power with non-Muslims, which is something Muslims in no country have ever done. They have either ruled over non-Muslims or been ruled by the latter.

To be able to take advantage of this opportunity, which has been truly available to them additionally by virtue of the nature of Hindu society, Muslims had to overcome, to begin with, the trauma and shame of partition. In this regard, they have shown remarkable resilience. They overcame the trauma a long time ago and it is now impossible to find a Muslim who feels guilty on account of his community's role in the division of the country. This, however, could not have sufficed, and has not sufficed, to enable them to share power with others in the democratic political order. By and large, Muslims have accepted a passive patron-client relationship with those in office; they have not sought to participate actively in the political process by trying to share leadership.

No political party has succeeded in making Muslims partners in the common enterprise of building a secular and democratic India. Muslims, as a *community* do not, and, indeed, cannot accept secularism as a legitimate doctrine for the public domain. For them the public domain is not separate from the all-encompassing religious realm. This problem haunts the entire *ummah* and not only its Indian constituent; it is first and above all a community of believers.

Finally, with the disintegration of the Soviet state, Islam is the only important collectivist ideology to survive in the twentieth century. In no Muslim country can the philosophy of liberalism be said to be in the ascendant. In fact, if anything, the hold of the collectivist approach has increased in recent years. That is what Islamic fundamentalism represents.

That reality inevitably impinges on Indian Muslims, including the intelligentsia. There is, however, a difference in the Indian Muslim situation as it obtained before partition and as it obtains now.

Advocacy of *jihad* (holy war), for example, is out of the question in India in view of the correlation of forces. Muslim leaders, such as they are, cannot now invoke the concept of *ijma* (consensus) as their predecessors could and did before 1947. No organization or individual can claim to embody such a consensus as the Muslim League and Jinnah could. In addition, the present Muslim leaders cannot, in today's India, pour ridicule on the politics of numbers as men like Sir Sayyid Ahmed Khan could.

To put it differently, even the most adventurist and irrational Muslim cannot question the legitimacy of the political order based on the Constitution, which, in turn, rests on the right of the individual. Many of them are, in reality, opposed to individualism and therefore liberalism and secularism; all three are products of one large revolution. But they cannot bring this opposition into the open since these assure for the community participation in the political process and enable it to preserve and even strengthen its identity. In plain terms, Muslims have no option but to accept the status quo, and, by and large, they do.

The concepts of democracy and secularism can, in theory, threaten to disrupt the community by encouraging individualism and challenge to *ijma*. In reality, they do not. The liberal challenge from both within and without remains and is likely to remain feeble for the foreseeable future. The secularism-pseudo-secularism debate has been and remains a non-Muslim, indeed, essentially, an intra-Hindu affair; so does the desirability or otherwise of a common civil code. The Muslim community has drawn a great 'China Wall' around itself which cannot be easily breached.

The Nehruvian Framework

As discussed earlier, two processes have been on among Hindus since the early nineteenth century — modernization and self-renewal. Of the two processes modernization has in a sense been stronger. For one thing, behind modernization has stood the appeal and power of the dominant Western civilization, which has been all-encompassing as no other has ever been. For another, it has plainly been out of the question to organize the economy and polity on a non-Western basis. All attempts to conceptualize an alternative, beginning with Gandhiji and ending with Jayaprakash Narayan in the 1970s, have come a cropper. For our purpose, the power and appeal of modernization is best illustrated by the easy sway Pandit Nehru acquired in the wake of independence.

Nehru was Gandhiji's lieutenant and heir-designate during the freedom movement. But he stood for a very different India from the master's and, as independence approached, he left the latter in no doubt that he was determined to have his way. The letters exchanged between them on the eve of independence speak volumes. Nehru was dismissive of the Mahatma's approach as outlined in *Hind Swaraj* (1908) and the Mahatma acquiesced in it virtually without protest, though it may be recalled, Gandhiji had taken the initiative in raising the question of what kind of India was to be built on achievement of freedom, emphasizing that he still stood by his old vision. Gandhiji did not reply to the issues raised by Nehru.

Perhaps he realized that he had played his role. Regardless, however, of whether he realized it or not, the time was truly up for him. This is not to deny either his heroic role in the struggle to contain passions unleashed by partition or the historic importance of his martyrdom. But, in the final analysis, that only facilitated Nehru's pre-eminence and the downgrading of his only potential rival, Sardar Patel, who, incidentally, was no Gandhian either.

The Sardar had better insight (not just administrative and organizational skill) into India's needs. But the atmosphere was not propitious for him precisely because the Hindu element in his personality was stronger than the modernist with its emphasis on socialism and secularism as articulated by not only Nehru but also other leaders such as Jayaprakash Narayan and Ram Manohar Lohia who had come into prominence in the 1942 Quit India Movement. Thus while Gandhism and Gandhians have been a marginal phenomenon in independent India, Nehru continues to dominate the thinking of the Indian intelligentsia three decades after his death. Modernizers are still in command.

Nehru's role in the modernization of India is well known. There is, however, another face of Nehru which places him, even if indirectly, among the proponents of Hindu civilization. This, of course, is not one of Nehru's prominent faces. He rarely allowed it to come to the fore. But unlike most of his followers, Nehru was deeply involved with the problem of the cultural-civilizational personality of India.

Nehru himself spoke and wrote extensively for well over four decades. Much of what he wrote as Prime Minister between 1947 and 1964 is still not available for scrutiny. As such, we have to rely primarily on S. Gopal's assessment of him as spelt out in his three-volume study of Nehru.[1] So far, no one else has been allowed full access to the Nehru papers. There is, however, evidence to show that somewhere at the back of Nehru's mind lurked reservation regarding the path on which he had helped launch India. Though this evidence is available publicly in the collection of his speeches, it has been neglected.

This is particularly surprising because it is well known that Nehru struggled to discover the soul of India as no other Indian public figure did; Gandhiji's struggle was of an altogether different kind, though it was far more valiant. Nehru was handicapped in a variety of ways. He did not know Sanskrit, or for that matter, any Indian language well enough. He did not have direct access to Indian tradition even by way of folklore since Motilal Nehru had deliberately Westernized himself and brought up Jawaharlal in a manner appropriate to an English gentleman. He was educated at Eton and Harrow. Nehru was essentially not a deep thinker. To the extent he was interested in ideas, he was familiar only with ideas current in Britain in his impressionable years; Fabian socialism, for instance.

Above all, he approached India's past, historical as well as spiritual, through British scholars who inevitably saw India through their culturally coloured prisms. Western scholarship was also in its infancy. Much more valuable work was done when Nehru was too deeply involved in public affairs to keep track of it. As it happened, the more valuable work was done by French and German Orientalists who were not accessible to him on account of the language barrier. Many of us still encounter this difficulty.

Nehru's intellectual background led him to take a synthetic (aggregationist) view of Indian culture, though on a more careful reflection, it should have been possible for him to recognize, on the one hand, its integral unity founded on yoga, of which the Veda itself is a fruit, and, on the other, its capaciousness on the strength of the same boundless yogic foundation which placed no limit on the freedom of the human spirit. Inevitably this synthetic view of Indian culture led him — especially in view of the Persianized cultural background of his own forebears and of the Kashmiri Pandit community in the plains and, indeed, in the valley itself — to accept the theory of a Hindu-Muslim cultural synthesis. The fact of partition must have provoked some doubt in his mind. He was too sensitive and honest an individual not to be shaken by so traumatic a development.

But, by then, it was too late for him to review and restate his basic position, even if he were so inclined. No political leader in his position could afford to do so. And if it was too late before partition, it was certainly worse after independence when he was charged with the task of covering up the wounds inflicted by the Muslim League in the hope that the cover-up would allow the healing process to take over in course of time. All that makes it truly remarkable that he allowed himself to say as much as he did. Three of his speeches deserve attention in this regard. The first of these was his address to the convocation of the Aligarh Muslim University on 24 January 1948. In it he said:

> I am proud of India, not only because of her ancient, magnificent heritage, but also because of her remarkable capacity to add to it by keeping the doors and windows of her mind and spirit open to fresh and invigorating winds from distant lands. India's strength has been twofold: her own innate culture which flowered through the ages, and her capacity to

draw from other sources and thus add to her own. She was far too strong to be submerged by outside streams, and she was too wise to isolate herself from them, and so there is a continuing synthesis in India's real history, and the many political changes which have taken place have had little effect on the growth of this variegated and yet essentially unified culture.

I have said that I am proud of our inheritance and our ancestors who gave an intellectual and cultural pre-eminence to India. How do you feel about this past? Do you feel that you are also sharers in it and inheritors of it and, therefore, proud of something that belongs to you as much as to me? Or do you feel alien to it and pass it by without understanding it or feeling that strange thrill which comes from the realization that we are the trustees and inheritors of this vast treasure....You are Muslims and I am a Hindu. We may adhere to different religious faiths or even to none; but that does not take away from that cultural inheritance that is yours as well as mine.

In view of his bitter experience of events leading to partition, it is inconceivable that Nehru could be so naïve as to believe even vaguely that educated Muslims could possibly regard themselves as 'sharers and inheritors' of the cultural heritage he was speaking about. In fact, it would be reasonable to infer that he said what he did precisely because he knew that the opposite was true.

Nehru posed another question to his audience: "Do we believe in a national State which includes people of all religions...and is essentially secular as a State, or do we believe in the religious, theocratic conception of a State which regards people of other faiths as somebody beyond the pale?" He, of course, did not remind them that only a few months earlier many of them had sympathized with, if not actively worked for, Pakistan. But he did speak of "one national outlook" which would inform the working of the Indian state, though he did not spell out the source for the development of that "one national outlook."[2]

In a different way and in a different context, though, Nehru expanded on this theme. In his address at the inauguration of the Indian Council for Cultural Relations in New Delhi on 9 April 1950, he said:

> One can see each nation and each separate civilization developing its own culture that had its roots in generations hundreds and thousands of years ago. One sees these nations being intimately moulded by the impulse that initially starts a civilization going on its long path. That conception is affected by other conceptions and one sees action and interaction between these varying conceptions.
>
> Culture, if it has to have any value, must have a certain depth. It must also have a certain dynamic character. If we leave out what might be called the basic mould that was given to it in the early stages of a people's growth, it is affected by geography, by climate and by all kinds of other factors. The culture of Arabia is intimately governed by the geography and the deserts of Arabia because it grew up there. Obviously, the culture of India in the old days was affected greatly, as we see in our literature, by the Himalayas, the forests and the great rivers of India among other things. It was a natural growth from the soil....
>
> The individual human being or race or nation must necessarily have a certain depth and certain roots somewhere. They do not count for much unless they have roots in the past, which past is after all the accumulation of generations of experience and some type of wisdom. It is essential that you have that. Otherwise you become just pale copies of something which has no real meaning to you as an individual or as a group.... [3]

This emphasis on roots, depth, past, basic mould and soil must come as a surprise to all those who are not familiar with this little known face of Nehru. It must also raise the question why he did not develop this theme and indeed why he kept this face of his, by and large, so well covered? Many answers are possible.

The last of the three addresses I have in view was the Azad memorial lecture Nehru delivered on 22 February 1959. He said:

When Islam came to India in the form of political conquest it brought conflict; it encouraged the tendency of Hindu society to shrink still further within its shell. Hence the great problem that faced India during the medieval period was how these two closed systems, each with its strong roots, could develop a healthy relationship.

The philosophy and the world outlook of the old Hindus was amazingly tolerant. The Muslims had to face a new problem, namely, how to live with others as equals. They came into conflict with Christendom and through hundreds of years the problem was never solved. In India, slowly a synthesis was developed. But before this could be completed, other influences came into play.[4]

Typically, Nehru skirts inconvenient issues. He does not tell us why the Christian-Muslim encounter did not lead to a synthesis despite the common Semitic origins of the two faiths, or how Hindus and Muslims could move towards one if both were truly closed systems, or why Hindus shrank into their shell before the onslaught of Islam since they had not faced a hostile civilization earlier. He also uses the wrong concept of tolerance in relation to Hindus and Hinduism in place of the proper one, which is 'comprehensive' or 'all-embracing' or 'total'. Hindus were 'amazingly tolerant' because their *dharma* (worldview) provided for every possible expression of the human spirit and indeed they so remained in spite of their decline for centuries for the same reason.

We can, however, let all that pass. The statement is notable for us, on the one hand, for its admission that the Hindu-Muslim conflict had not been resolved when the British arrived on the scene to produce new complications, and, on the other, for its diagnosis of the cause of the Hindu decline and the cure. Nehru, as is well known, generally avoided the first and was preoccupied with the second problem. The same, incidentally, was true of the Mahatma, with the difference that while he saw a resolution of the problem in social reform, with heavy emphasis on removal of untouchability, Nehru regarded the development of science and technology through the mediation of a strong state and contact with the West, which for him included the Soviet Union, as the key to India's future.

Thus, it is possible to take the view that Nehru put aside the issue of the pre-eminence of Hindu civilization because he was convinced that Hindus needed first to overcome the weakness resulting from their lagging behind in the field of science and technology. It must be remembered that he grew up in Britain in the age of optimism before the First World War when the Western man entertained little doubt that limitless progress was possible, if not inevitable, and that science based on reason and technology were the instruments of that march into the future. Nehru, it may also be recalled, spoke frequently of the need to overcome 'superstition' and to cultivate the scientific temper. He did not identify Hindus as his target audience. But they *were* his target audience.

It is inconceivable that Nehru was not sensitive to Muslim resistance to modernization and secularization. Indeed, it can safely be assumed that he left them alone in respect of their Personal Law and did not seek to bring them into the orbit of a common civil code precisely because he was aware of the depth of their opposition, though that is clearly an essential part of a modern polity based on the principle of equal citizenship. Perhaps he expected that their attitude would change in course of time under the pressure of forces unleashed by the spread of education, economic development and the democratic political process. If he ever spelt out his views on how the Muslims would come out of their ghetto psychology after independence, it has still not been made public. Alternatively, it is possible that he was too busy managing the affairs of the state of India on a day-to-day basis to be able to pay attention to this problem. We just do not know Nehru's views on a long-term resolution of the Muslim question.

Nehru spoke often of the need for 'national integration'. But if he ever defined what that called for by way of change among Muslims in practical terms, I am not aware of it. The addresses quoted earlier do not contain any action programme. He denounced communalism. He was particularly harsh on what he called 'Hindu communalism' on the ground (as he explained in a letter to Dr. K.N. Katju, at one stage his home minister) that it would be far more dangerous in view of the power of Hindus in independent India. In reality, his perspective provided for nothing nobler than co-existence between Hindus and Muslims. His was basically a programme which would help avoid riots, which understandably revolted him as they did other sensitive Indians. Indeed, the policy of secularism cannot realistically be interpreted otherwise, the grandiose theories notwithstanding. It certainly did not provide, even in theory, for a cultural synthesis. It sought to bypass the civilizational-cultural issue altogether.

It is beyond question that no issue occupied so much of Nehru's time and energy as Kashmir. This was clearly an obsession with him so much so that it would be no exaggeration to say that he allowed his whole foreign policy to be heavily influenced by it. The reasons for this are complex and need not detain us in the present exercise. Three points may, however, be made in respect of his handling of the problem. First, having placed himself in a vulnerable position by offering to hold a plebiscite, he allowed himself to be blackmailed by Sheikh Abdullah. The evidence is overwhelming. The near independent status he conceded to Jammu and Kashmir violated his very concept of the kind of Indian state which could protect India's unity. It would be relevant to recall his opposition to Punjabi Suba in this connection. Similarly, the manner in which the Sheikh rigged the election to his Constituent Assembly could not but have caused the deepest hurt to Nehru. It negated his commitment to democracy.

Secondly, Nehru effectively used the Kashmir issue to silence his critics. It is truly remarkable that as India's position in the state became precarious, necessitating the overthrow and imprisonment of the Sheikh and maintenance, by New Delhi, in power in Srinagar of one corrupt regime after another, the more successful was Nehru in using the Kashmir card at home. Clearly, the Indian people acquiesced in this self-deception. The psychology behind this acquiescence needs to be explored. It has not been, to the best of my knowledge. It, however, seems to me that our presence in Kashmir served as a substitute for cultural self-assertion for Hindus, especially for the Western-educated elite engaged, *albeit* unconsciously, in a desperate search for an ersatz substitute. In plain terms, Nehru or no Nehru, we have not been ready for a genuine cultural self-affirmation.

Finally, once he had accepted, whether of his own volition or under coercion, a constitutional arrangement for Kashmir which would preserve the 'identity' of Kashmiri Muslims, above all a product of their relative isolation from the rest of the country on account of geographical factors, he had also acknowledged, even if only by implication that he could not use the Kashmir 'experiment' to promote a change in the attitude of Muslims in the rest of the Indian Union. This brings me to the point I made earlier regarding Nehru's lack of confidence in his ability to persuade Muslims to get out of the psychological and cultural ghetto of their own making and join the mainstream brought forth, in his view, by the process of modernization. It does not follow that Nehru's secularism was phoney; but it does mean that it was lame. To borrow the Chinese phrase, it did not walk on two legs. It wobbled on one, though Muslims provided him a crutch in the shape of electoral support which facilitated his and the Congress party's stay in power.

The Nehru order, however, did not rest on the secular pillar alone. It would have collapsed long ago if it had. The Nehru structure has stood mainly on three pillars in conceptual terms – socialism, secularism and non-alignment – and these concepts have been interlinked. Nehru's was an integrated worldview. As such, it is only logical that if one of them becomes dysfunctional, the others must get into trouble. In my opinion, they have.

Socialism was clearly central to Nehru's worldview. For, it shaped his views on nationalism, democracy, secularism and non-alignment as well. Nehru, it may be recalled, was the first Congress leader to define nationalism in terms of anti-imperialism and link anti-imperialism to the Soviet leadership's effort to fight capitalism both at home and abroad. No significant non-

Marxist Congress leader bought this proposition when Nehru began to propound it in the twenties because they were opposed to socialism at home. But they could not produce an alternative definition of nationalism for the simple reason that they could not explicitly link it with the country's cultural past for fear of offending the Muslims. So, finally, Nehru's formulations prevailed. The triumph became complete when he came to dominate both the ruling party (after Sardar Patel's death in 1950) and the government and gave an anti-Western tilt to the country's foreign policy in the name of non-alignment.

It is possible that Nehru, a man of moderation, would not have gone as far as he did if, for one thing, Krishna Menon, who had spent much of his adult life in London amidst socialists of different varieties, had not come to exercise enormous influence on him and if, for another, the West under Britain's inspiration had not tilted towards Pakistan on the Kashmir issue.

It follows that the concept of secular nationalism more or less divorced from the country's cultural heritage could not have been a viable proposition if it was not girded by the promise of a brave new socialist world of equality. As far as I know, Nehru never spoke of creating a new Indian. Mother India stuck to him as he said she stuck to every Indian whatever he may do or think. On account of the same restraint, he did not think in terms of dragooning India into the socialist Utopia as Stalin did in the Soviet Union and Mao Zedong in China. There was also another side to his personality which linked him to India's past. He was more than a deeply moral human being. He yearned for spiritual light. He was particularly drawn to Swami Vivekanand and the Ramakrishna Ashram. It is known that he sought solace from Anandmai to whom Indira Gandhi also turned. Once he visited Sri Aurobindo Ashram as well and met The Mother. Dr. S. Radhakrishnan, President of the Indian

Republic, disclosed that in the last years of his life, Nehru used to come to him frequently to listen to the Upanishads which, as *The Discovery of India* shows, always fascinated him. Even so, it cannot be denied that his programme was intended to produce a new Indian in the style of the new Soviet man or China man.

For Nehru, freedom was meaningful mainly if it paved the way for economic growth. He said so publicly again and again. Similarly, for him, democracy was meaningful if it facilitated movement towards economic and social equality. His was a commitment not so much to liberal democracy which prizes liberty more than equality as to democratic socialism which reverses the order of priorities. Nehru did not play havoc with the Constitution in his search for socialism. He was too imbued with the spirit of liberalism to do that. It could not occur to him that non-democratic means would be justified in the pursuit of socialism. But by emphasizing equality and, in the process, undermining the concept of the liberty of the individual, he created an atmosphere in which it became possible for his successors, Indira Gandhi foremost among them, to play with the Constitution and the constitutional arrangement. The emergency would have been inconceivable if demagogues, sired by Nehru, however unwittingly, had not prepared the ground.

This, however, takes us too far afield. I am here interested in establishing that socialism, however vaguely defined and implemented, was the linchpin of the Nehru system and that the system cannot possibly survive the disappearance of this linchpin. The linchpin has clearly disappeared. The collapse of the Soviet system and state and the opening of the Chinese economy to multinationals would by themselves have settled the issue. As it happens, the threat of bankruptcy as a result of the mismanagement of the economy since the very start of planning in the early fifties and more particularly in recent years has forced the Government of India to make a volte-face. It has abandoned all the dogmas and shibboleths of the Nehru-Indira Gandhi era. And the irony of it is that a Congress (I) government is presiding over this great reversal.

I am not unaware of the fact that this is not the popular interpretation of Nehru. And I cannot possibly insist that this is more valid than the popular one. Indeed I could not have put it forward if I had not become sensitive to the concept of the power of the time spirit in recent months. This has led me to the conclusion that much more could not have been successfully attempted by way of reaffirmation of Hindu civilization in the period in question.

It is not particularly relevant to speculate on the 'ifs' and 'buts' of history. So, I would not wish to speculate on what turn India could have taken if Sardar Patel, or C. Rajagopalachari, or Rajendra Prasad had taken over as prime minister in place of Nehru, except to say that each of them would have been out of tune with the dominant sentiment in the Third World and among the Indian intelligentsia.

The real, as Hegel said, is rational. Things are what they are because in the given interplay of forces, they could not possibly have shaped differently. And it is the correlation of forces that shapes history not ideology. On the contrary, an ideology itself is a product of those forces. On this reckoning, our cultural-civilizational reaffirmation had to await the collapse of communism and its Third World expressions such as Arab nationalism, and the acquisition of a certain measure of scientific, technological, economic and military strength by us. Islamic revivalism-fundamentalism is, of course, not a direct offshoot of communism; it antedates the latter by centuries. But in the post-war era it has been as critically dependent on Soviet power as has been pan-Arabian.

Thus, it is possible to think of Hindu self-affirmation and self-renewal as a process to which Gandhiji and Nehru contributed considerably and to conclude that L.K. Advani, with his quiet but confident assertion of the primacy of Hindus and Hinduism in India, fits in this unfolding progression. Advani too can ask Muslims the same questions Nehru posed at Aligarh in 1948.

The fact that the Nehru order was under strain since the Chinese attack in 1962 and in visible decline in recent years is seldom recalled in the public discourse on the Ramjanambhoomi issue. But that only shows how lopsided the discourse is.

The Chinese attack knocked down two myths: one, that communist states do not commit aggression which is supposed to be the peculiarity of imperialism, and two, that the policy of peaceful co-existence could help avoid the need for military preparedness. If it were not for the bitter dispute between the Soviet Union and China, which obliged Moscow to befriend New Delhi, it would have put paid to the policy of non-alignment as such. That, however, only postponed the demise. It materialized in 1989, when the Soviet Union itself disintegrated.

Nehruvian socialism has been in deep trouble for quarter of a century. By 1967, it was obvious, except to Marxists and fellow travellers, that all that it had done was to have spawned a regime of corruption, slowed down economic growth, degraded the country's public life and generated enormous tension in society.

The pursuit of these two policies has been a reflection of the partial nature of the Hindu recovery. A more confident Hindu psyche would never have spurned the US offer of cooperation [President Eisenhower's offer in 1954 of 'proportionate' military assistance, proportionate that is, to India's size, importance and potentiality, in comparison to Pakistan, with which the US had then concluded a mutual security pact and embraced the illusion of friendship with China in the occupation of Tibet. China 'repaid' Nehru with (1) demands on Indian territory in disregard of the internationally recognized watershed – the highest mountain range principle; (2) friendship with Pakistan; and (3) an outright attack on India in 1962] and allowed Pakistan to seek military parity with, if not superiority over, this country. Similarly, such a psyche would never have reconciled itself to an economic philosophy which would stunt the growth of the agricultural as well as the business community.

This un-Hindu disregard for power, economic and military, and the illusory belief that social equity is possible in conditions of economic weakness is also the product of minds nurtured in the tradition of Chaitanya's Bhakti movement which Bankim Chandra Chatterjee criticized in *Anandmath*. It is not an accident either that this tradition among Hindus has weakened since independence, as Hindus have grappled with the problems of the state, as it weakened among the Sikhs when they battled the Mughals and the Afghans, or that it is invoked by all those who swear by a 'composite culture' and are alarmed at the reintroduction of the Kshatriya element in the urban Hindu's personality. In my view, the second phase of the freedom struggle, 'the struggle to regain its Hindu identity', will involve a reconstitution of the fragmented Hindu personality along lines different from the one pursued so far, so that the missing Kshatriya constituent of the old Hindu personality is restored. As for secularism, supposedly the third leg of the Nehruvian tripod, two points have to be made. The first is the usual one, which is that Hinduism is tolerant and, therefore, secular. This is valid and it is sheer dishonesty or naïveté to suggest, as is being widely suggested these days, that Hinduism can admit of theocracy. That is a Muslim privilege which no one else can appropriate.

Secondly, the dominant concern of Hindus over the last 200 years has been with achievements in the secular realm — education, trade, industry, equality with the British before independence and with the West since independence. The upsurge I have been speaking about, in fact, relates wholly to the secular realm. This does not mean that our spiritual-religious heritage has no place in this scheme. But it does mean that Hindus have recognized once again, as they did in the past, that the secular realm has to be secured if a culture and a civilization has to flourish. Swami Vivekanand emphasized the importance of secular achievements and so did Sri Aurobindo.

Society and culture, it need hardly be said, are interlinked. Social changes brought about by secular forces are duly reflected in culture in course of time. That has been happening in the case of Hinduism. It is not being Semitized and it cannot be Semitized as a result of a deliberate design on the part of some individuals or groups. But from being a confederation of ways of life, it has had to move towards being a federation. To put it differently, the small society has had to give way to larger ones as small economies and polities have had to give way to larger ones. Only a secular and modern intelligentsia could have presided over these changes. The task would have been beyond the reach of traditional elites. That is the true significance of secularism. It may be called the 'midwife of Hindu nationalism'.

The concept of secularism and the secularization process have, of course, not been a Hindu monopoly.

Members of other religious groups have also pursued them but essentially as individuals. Muslims as a group have certainly shunned the concept as well as the process to the extent they can in a larger modernizing and, therefore, secularizing society. This is evident from the rapid expansion of traditional mosque-attached *madrasahs* (schools), opposition to one common civil code and adherence to the Shariat. Faith can never be a private affair for most Muslims. As such, political parties and leaders have to woo them as Muslims. This has inevitably produced a backlash of which the Ramjanambhoomi issue has become one major expression.

I do not criticize Muslims for their reluctance and even refusal to take to the secularization process. Nor can I applaud Hindus for their participation in this process. For while the spirit of liberalism and pluralism, which the West represents, is alien to Islam, as it has developed since the eleventh century when the orthodox ulema triumphed over philosophers, Sufis and other kinds of innovators, they are in conformity with Hinduism which revels in plurality. But this divergence creates a serious problem for both which the self-proclaimed secularists have refused steadfastly to face.

Finally, it is a pity that there does not exist the slightest awareness, either among Hindus or Muslims, that Muslims need the rise of Indian civilization as much as Hindus, if not more. Indeed, such is the grip of the misrepresentation of Hindutva in anti-Muslim terms that its proponents, including some leaders of the Bharatiya Janata Party, themselves, speak of it defensively.

History knows of any number of instances when a community has needed to be protected, or liberated, from, its own 'leaders': Germans under Hitler; Russians under Stalin; Chinese under Mao Zedong; and, more recently Iraqis under Saddam Hussain, for example. Hitler and Saddam Hussain first let loose a reign of terror at home and broke the spirit of their own peoples before they went to war with other countries. Indeed, the war at home is central to all dictators. Stalin got an opportunity to extend his tyrannical rule to eastern Europe only towards the end of the Second World War. Earlier he, like Mao later, had to be 'content' with mass massacres at home, and he was about to return to that 'sport' at the time of his death in 1953. To extend the argument further, while the West has doubtless celebrated the collapse of communist tyrannies in eastern Europe, the principal beneficiaries have been the peoples of those unhappy lands.

Indian Muslims, I am convinced, after many years of reflection, too, like Hindus, need self-renewal; unlike Hindus, they have proved incapable of engaging in such an exercise even under the stimulus provided by British rule, and only the triumph of Hindutva can help create a milieu which obliges them to try and overcome the inertia of tradition reinforced by the ulema.

I must confess that, like many others, I too have tended to think in terms of leaving Muslims to their ghetto mentality, and to oppose the demand, by BJP leaders, among others, for a uniform civil code. My argument has been that so large and obstinate a community cannot be pushed against its will, that any attempt to do so would aggravate existing tensions and that such a risk should best be avoided. I have also had no reason either to believe that 'modernizers' in the community are anything but an utterly marginal phenomenon or to dispute that the ulema continue to represent it. That, incidentally, was also why I was not opposed to the scandalous piece of legislation known as the Muslim Women (Protection of Rights on Divorce) Act which, in fact, denies even utterly destitute Muslim divorcees in danger of becoming vagrants the right to alimony from their former husbands.

Incidentally, this attitude is also proof that our secularism has become a euphemism for callous indifference to the fate of Muslims. V.P. Singh and others may woo them in their search for power, but they cannot offer them a way out of the ghetto mentality. The BJP offers them such a way, though it too does not know the glorious implications for Muslims of the Hindutva platform and harps on the old demand for a common civil code.

A common civil code can be, indeed is, part of a nationalist platform which, on the one hand, demands that all citizens live under the same laws, and, on the other, entitles Parliament, or any other legally constituted body, to enact such laws for all citizens. But it cannot figure prominently in the Hindutva platform which must, by its very nature determined by the Hindu civilization's unlimited catholicity and broadmindedness, seek to influence by way of example and not engage in coercion. The Hindu temperament also militates against uniformity and coercion. Unlike Muslims, Hindus have never sought to fix a mould in which Hindu personality must be shaped. Indeed, in the case of Brahmins, the personality shaped by the tradition of memorizing texts is yielding place to a different one, better attuned to critical analysis. Pandit Nehru could recite no Sanskrit *shloka*. That apart, however, the proponents of 'secular nationalism' cannot sidetrack certain questions. Since they too cannot deny that Muslims, on the whole, have remained frozen in their attitudes, as illustrated by their passionate adherence to the Muslim Personal Law, they owe it to themselves to explain why this remains the case after more than four decades of life under a secular political order, and what they propose to do to end this stagnation. They should not beat about the bush and indulge in tirades against Hindu 'communalism', or fascism, or whatever new term of abuse they can borrow from the West; for they also cannot be so ridiculous as to argue that it in any way accounts for the prevalence of the ghetto mentality among Muslims.

It is common knowledge that, if anything, the revivalist, fundamentalist sentiment among Muslims has become stronger in the past decade or so when hundreds of millions of petrodollars have poured in from Saudi Arabia, Libya and other oil-rich countries, and that the terrorist menace we now face in Kashmir is one offshoot of this revivalist-fundamentalist upsurge. For, it cannot be disputed that the Jamaat-i-Islami played a key role in whipping up initially an anti-India hysteria in the valley and that hundreds of *madrasahs* under its control, generously financed by its patrons abroad, have provided the recruiting ground for Pakistan-backed terrorists and secessionists.

I understand from Muslim reformists, a rare species, that the position of poor Muslim women has deteriorated as a result of the Muslim Women (Protection of Rights on Divorce) Act, which Rajiv Gandhi pushed through Parliament in 1986 under pressure from the ulema, because it has taken away from them what little protection Section 125 of the Criminal Procedure Code had given them earlier. This may or may not be the case. The condition of poor Muslim women has been too bad to deteriorate much further. But it is indisputable that Hizb-i-Islamia, an underground outfit in Jammu and Kashmir, has forced even educated Muslim women to return to the burqa. No secularist Hindu is likely to lose his sleep on such an insignificant development! But they cannot deny that this constitutes a violation of the spirit of rights conferred by the Constitution as much on Muslim women as on anyone else.

It is sheer escapism and worse (dishonesty) to talk of bride burning or maltreatment of women among Hindus in this specific context. Apart from the undeniable fact that Hindu women are coming into their own in millions as a result of education and employment outside the home, laws exist and more stringent ones can be enacted to deal with such problems among Hindus. Muslim women cannot be given similar protection under the existing dispensation. Moreover, no one can possibly suggest that Hindus have insulated themselves from the winds of change. On the contrary, Hindu society is being, as it were, reconstituted and there is no organized resistance to it.

One of the greatest problems of Hindu society, and, by that logic, of Indian society, is the fragmentation of the Hindu social order into more and more castes. Inevitably, our fundamental struggle is to restore a kind of unity, without which, it makes little sense to talk of Hinduism. We have to produce a sense of coherence in an order which has become, over the centuries, increasingly fragmented and chaotic. All our social movements in the last 200 years and all our political movements in the last 100 years should be seen in that context. So viewed they would not look divisive and, therefore, unhealthy. I do not, for instance, regard Kanshi Ram and the Bahujan Samaj Party which he has launched as a disaster in spite of his spiteful attacks on Brahmins who have helped preserve our heritage under extremely trying circumstances. This is part of a larger struggle to reverse the process of fragmentation and restore the original *chaturvarna* (fourfold) order to the extent it is viable in the present context. The struggle is going to be long and painful. It requires large minds and large hearts to be able to accommodate so many currents which are addressed to a common purpose, the common purpose being a new sense of coherence, a new sense of unity without break in continuity.

It would be premature yet to sound an optimistic note, but I sense, even if still vaguely, the possibility of a profound change in Indian Muslims also. The issues involved in this formulation are clearly too many and too complex. So, I will limit myself to a few observations.

First, no worthwhile attempt has been made for decades to define Indian nationalism in *Indian* terms for the simple reason that no one has been able to accommodate the Muslim factor within the framework of Hindu civilization. Nehru talked of a Hindu-Muslim cultural synthesis but one has only to refer to his address to the Aligarh Muslim University in 1948 and to the Indian Council for Cultural Relations in 1950 (mentioned earlier) to know that he came to entertain serious reservations about it.

Secondly, the Indian intellectual-political elite sought to fill the void arising out of the absence of a conscious articulation of a nationalist ideology with the talk of secularism. This strategy worked for so long on two counts. First, there existed, in the Congress, an organization which could represent Hindu aspirations in the secular realm and treat Muslims as its clients in all but name. Second, the Hindu recovery of self-confidence and, therefore, need for self-affirmation in civilizational terms was of an order that it could be accommodated within the Congress framework.

Surely, these conditions no longer obtain. The Congress has grown weak over the years; with the arrival of the Janata Dal and its offshoots on the scene, Muslims have got another option and therefore want to be wooed rather than treated as clients; and, above all, Hindu recovery, going back to the eighteenth century, has finally acquired such power and momentum that it cannot be content to operate in disguise which is all that was possible under the Congress umbrella. So they have erected their own institutional arrangements with the Rashtriya Swayamsevak Sangh as the base and the BJP, the VHP and other organizations as its arms.

Thirdly, a series of developments — the collapse of pan-Arabism, or Arab nationalism, symbolized currently by the defeat of Saddam Hussain's Iraq; return of Western powers to the Gulf; disappearance of a rival anti-US power centre in Moscow; renewed tensions between Sunni-dominated Baghdad and Shia Iran; failure of the Islamic revolution in Iran to justify itself in terms of results; and the power struggle in Tehran — must create for Indian Muslims a psychological situation the like of which they have not faced. Since the beginning of the decline of the Mughal empire in the early eighteenth century, a critical point for Indian Islam, there has existed for them a centre of hope and reference. No such reference-hope centre exists now.

Leaving aside the implications of the rise of the RSS-BJP-VHP combine as a significant factor in Indian politics, it is about time we pay attention to the hitherto neglected question of the impact of Hindi on Muslim youth in North India. For all we know, a return, even if slow, to one-culture situation may have begun. The process cannot but be prolonged and painful and the pace may not be good enough for modernists. But obsession with speed is alien to Indian civilization which under-writes the Indian nation-state.

I for one see no alternative to it. This is my view of the place of Muslims in India — one strand in the multistrand Indian civilization interacting with others. This is also my interpretation of what Pandit Nehru meant by cultural synthesis. Only he did not attach to language the importance I do.

6

Ayodhya: A Historical Watershed

1992 will doubtless go down in Indian history as the *year of Ayodhya*. This is so not so much because recent events there have pushed into the background all other issues such as economic reforms and reservations for the 'other backward castes' as because they have released forces which will have a decisive influence in shaping the future of India.

These forces are not new; they have been at work for two centuries. Indeed, they were not even wholly bottled up. But they had not been unleashed earlier as they have been now. It is truly extraordinary that the demolition of a nondescript structure by faceless men no organization owns up should have shaken so vast a country as India. But no one can possibly deny that it has. These forces in themselves are not destructive even if they have led to some violence and blood-letting. They are essentially beneficent. They shall seek to heal the splits in the Indian personality so that it is restored to health and vigour.

Implicit in the above is the proposition that while India did not cease to be India either under Muslim or British rule despite all the trials and tribulations, she was not fully Mother India. And she was not fully Mother India not because she was called upon to digest external inputs, which is her nature to assimilate, but because she was not free to throw out what she could not possibly digest in the normal and natural course. This lack of freedom to reject what cannot be assimilated is the essence of foreign conquest and rule. The meaning of Ayodhya is that India has regained, to a larger extent than hitherto, the capacity to behave and act as a normal living organism. She has taken another big step towards self-affirmation.

All truth, as Lenin said, is partisan. So is mine. I do not pretend to be above the battle, or, to rephrase Pandit Nehru, I am not neutral against myself. But partisan truth is not demagogy and patently false propaganda, which is what advocates of 'composite culture' have engaged in. Two points need to be noted in this regard.

First, no living culture is ever wholly autonomous; for no *culture* is an airtight sealed box; Indian culture, in particular, has been known for its catholicity and willingness to give as well as take. It withdrew into a shell when it felt gravely threatened and became rigid; but that is understandable; indeed, the surprise, if any, is that Indian culture survived the Islamic and Western onslaught at all.

Secondly, a culture, if it is not swallowed up by an incoming one, whether by way of proselytization or conquest or both, as the Egyptians and Iranians were by Islam, or if it is not destroyed as the Aztec was by the Portuguese and the Spaniards, must seek to recover; even Indians in Latin America have not given up the effort. Surely, since no one can possibly suggest that Indian culture was either swallowed up or destroyed; it is only natural that it should seek to recover its genuine self. Surely, this is neither an anti-Islamic nor anti-Western activity.

Pandit Nehru almost never used the phrase 'composite culture'. His was a more organic view of culture and civilization. He believed in, and spoke of, cultural synthesis which, if at all, could take place only within the old civilizational framework since Islam did not finally triumph. Pandit Nehru also wrote and spoke of the spirit of India asserting itself again and again. Surely, that spirit could not be a composite affair. In the Maulana Azad memorial lecture (mentioned earlier) he also spoke of different cultures being products of different environments and he specifically contrasted tropical India with the deserts of Arabia. He even said that a Hindu-Muslim cultural synthesis had not been completed when other factors intervened. Apparently he was referring to the British Raj.

This should help dispel the impression that the Nehru era was a continuation of alien rule intended to frustrate the process of Indianization of India. This charge is not limited to his detractors. It is made by his admirers as well, though, of course, indirectly and unknowingly. They pit secularism against Hinduism which is plainly absurd. Hindus do not need the imported concept of secularism in order to be able to show respect towards other faiths. That comes naturally to them. For theirs is an inclusive faith which provides for every form of religious experience and belief; there can be no heresy or *kufr* in Hinduism.

For Nehru, secularism, both as a personal philosophy and state policy, was an expression of India's cultural-civilizational personality and not its negation and repudiation. Secularism suited India's requirements as he saw them. For instance, it provided an additional legitimizing principle for reform movements among Hindus beginning with the Brahmo Samaj in the early part of the nineteenth century. It met the aspirations of the Westernized and modernizing intelligentsia. Before independence, it denied legitimacy to Muslim separatism in the eyes of Hindus, Westernized or traditionalist. If it did not help forge an instrument capable of resisting effectively the Muslim League's demand for partition, the alternative platform of men such as Veer Savarkar did not avail either. After partition, it served the same purpose of denying legitimacy to moves to consolidate Muslims as a separate communalist political force.

Pandit Nehru's emphasis on secularism has to be viewed not only in relation to the Muslim problem which survived partition, but it has also to be seen in the context of his plea for science and of India's need to get rid of the heavy and deadening burden of rituals and superstitions, products of periods of grave weakness and hostile environment when nothing nobler than survival was possible. Seen in this perspective, the ideologies of socialism and secularism have served as mine sweepers. They have cleared the field of dead conventions sufficiently to make it possible for new builders to move in. Sheikh Abdullah exaggerated when he charged Pandit Nehru with Machiavellianism, but he was not too wide off the mark when he wrote in *Aatish-e-Chinar* that Nehru was "a great admirer of the past heritage and the Hindu spirit of India.... He considered himself as an instrument of rebuilding India with its ancient spirit" (quoted in Jagmohan, *My Frozen Turbulence in Kashmir*).[1]

The trouble is that self-styled Nehruites and other secularists are not able to recognize that India is no longer the convalescent she was not only when Gandhiji launched his first mass movement but also when she achieved independence with Pandit Nehru as the first prime minister. The two leaders have helped nurse her back to health as have their critics in different ways. That is the implication of my observation that the energies now unleashed have been at work for two centuries.

Only on a superficial view, resulting from a lack of appreciation of the history of modern India, beginning with Raja Rammohan Roy in the early nineteenth century, can the rise of the Ramjanambhoomi issue to its present prominence be said to be the result of a series of 'accidents': the sudden appearance of the Ramlalla idol in the structure in 1949 and the opening of the gate under the Faizabad magistrate's orders in 1986 being the most important. As in all such cases, these developments have helped bring out and reinforce something that was already growing – the 200-year-old movement for self-renewal and self-affirmation by Hindus. If this was not so, the 'accidents' in question would have petered out.

Similarly, while it cannot be denied that the RSS, the VHP, and the BJP have played a major role in mobilizing support for the cause of the temple, it should also be noted that they could not have achieved the success they have if the general atmosphere was not propitious and the time not ripe. Indeed, not to speak of Gandhiji who aroused and mobilized Hindus as no one had before him, fought the Christian missionary assault and successfully resisted the British imperialist designs to divide Harijans from Hindu society, it would be unfair to deny Nehru's and Indira Gandhi's contributions to the Hindu resurgence that we witness today. A civilizational revival, it may be pointed out, is a gradual, complex, and many-sided affair.

Again, only on the basis of a superficial view is it possible to see developments in India in isolation from developments in the larger world. Nehru's worldview, for instance, was deeply influenced by the socialist theories sweeping Europe in the wake of the First World War and the Soviet revolution in 1917. By the same token, this worldview, which has dominated our thinking for well over six decades, could not but become irrelevant in view of the collapse of communist regimes in eastern Europe, and the disarray in the Soviet Union itself. This cannot be seriously disputed even on rational grounds. Intensification of the search for identity in India today

is part of a similar development all over the world, especially in view of the collapse of communist 'universalism'.
But if it is a mere coincidence that the Ramjanambhoomi
issue has gathered support precisely in this period of the
disintegration of Soviet power abroad and the decline of
the Nehruvian consensus at home, it is an interesting one.

At the conscious level, the BJP, among political
formations, has chosen to be an instrument of India's
cultural and civilizational recovery and reaffirmation. As
such, it is natural that it will figure prominently in the
reshaping of India in the coming years and decades. But
others too will play their part in the gigantic enterprise.
V. P. Singh, for instance, has already rendered yeoman
service to the cause by undermining the social coalition
which has dominated the country's politics for most of the
period since independence.[2]

When a master idea seizes the mind, as socialism did
in the twenties, and as Hindutva has done now, it must
usher in radical change. In the twenties and the decades
that followed before and after independence, conservative
forces were not strong enough to resist the socialist idea.
Similarly, conservative forces are not strong enough today
to defeat the Hindutva ideal. There is a difference,
though, for while the socialist ideal related primarily to
economic reorganization and was elitist in its approach
by virtue of being a Western import, Hindutva seeks,
above all, to unleash the energies of a whole people which
foreign rule froze or drove underground.

When a historic change of this magnitude takes place,
intellectual confusion is generally unavoidable. The
human mind, as a rule, trails behind events; it is not
capable of anticipating them. But it should be possible
to cut through the mass of confusion and get to the heart
of the matter.

The heart of the matter is that if India's vast spiritual
(psychic in modern parlance) energies, largely dormant

for centuries, had to be tapped, Hindus had to be aroused; they could be aroused only by the use of a powerful symbol; that symbol could only be Ram, as was evident in the twenties when the Mahatma moved millions by his talk of Ramrajya; once the symbol takes hold of the popular mind, as Ram did in the twenties and as it has done now, opposition to it generally adds to its appeal.

An element of subjectivity and voluntarism, typical of a modern Westernized mind, has got introduced in the previous paragraph because that is the way I also think. In reality, the time spirit (*Mahakala*) unfolds itself under its own auspices, at its own momentum, as it were; we can either cooperate with it, or resist it at our peril.

Historians can continue to debate whether a temple, in fact, existed at the site of the Babri Masjid in Ayodhya; whether it was, in fact, a Ram temple; whether it was destroyed; or whether it had collapsed on its own. Similarly, moralists and secularists can go on arguing that it is not right to replace one place of worship by another, especially as long as the foregoing issues have not been resolved. But this is not how history moves and civilizational issues are settled.

Pertinent is the fact that for no other site have Hindus fought so bitterly for so long with such steadfastness as over Ramjanambhoomi in Ayodhya. There is no rational explanation for this and it is futile to look for one. All that is open to us is to grasp the fact and power of the mystery.

In all cultures and societies under great stress flows an invisible undercurrent. It does not always break surface. But when it does, it transforms the scene. This is how events in Ayodhya should be seen. The *Patal Ganga*, of which all Indians must have heard, has broken surface there. Human beings have doubtless played a part in this surfacing. But witness the remarkable fact that we do not know and, in fact, do not care who installed the Ramlalla idol in the Babri structure and who demolished the structure on 6 December 1992.

While almost everyone else is looking for scapegoats, to me it seems that every known actor is playing his or her allotted role in the vast drama that is being enacted. We are, as it were, witnessing the enactment of a modern version of Balmiki's Ramayana.

Resolving the Ancient Language Problem

An 'unknown' Indian has taken on proponents of Aryan invasion/migration theory, demolished their case, and established that northern India is the original home of the Indo-European family of languages. The importance of this remarkable achievement cannot be exaggerated. In course of time, it can compel the revision of the history not only of Indian but also world civilization.

The truth is invariably simple and convincing once one is able to cut through the maze of misinterpretation and obscurity. Indeed, one then wonders why other scholars could not grasp so obvious a proposition. This is so in the case of Srikant G. Telageri's *Aryan Invasion Theory and Indian Nationalism*.[1]

This is, of course, not the first conclusive repudiation of the invasion/migration theory in the English language. David Frawley too has made nonsense of it in his invaluable work *Gods, Sages and Kings: Vedic Secrets of Ancient Civilization*.[2] But he has not taken note in detail of what various proponents of the theory have written. The scope of his work is also much larger and in parts it is rather speculative. (Frawley is, incidentally, a recognized *Vedacharya* and has written extensively on various aspects of Vedic civilization.)

Telageri puts his finger at the source of much of the trouble when he challenges the common assumptions that the Vedic language was the earliest form of Indo-Aryan, that classical Sanskrit developed from the Vedic, that the Prakrits developed from Sanskrit, and the modern Indo-Aryan languages from these Prakrits.

According to him, the earliest from of Indo-European speech was spoken in the interior of India, in prehistoric times. It spread out as far north and west as Kashmir and Afghanistan; the original language developed into at least three Proto-languages: Proto-Outer-Indo-European (in northern Kashmir and Afghanistan), Proto-Central-Indo-European (in southern Kashmir and Punjab), and Proto-Inner Indo-European (in inner India).

This is Telageri's point of departure. And this is the crux of the matter. For if it can be established that the movement of the users of the Indo-European speech in India in ancient times was from the east to the west and not vice versa, the invasion/migration theory, as it has been propounded, cannot stand.

It is known to students of Sanskrit texts that they enumerate Indian rivers from the east to the west and not the other way around. But that evidence has not been regarded as strong enough. Telageri comes up with stronger evidence and the interesting point about it is that he locates it in the Rigveda itself.

One of the hymns of the Rigveda (IX. 96) and one of the three verses in another hymn (X. 179.2) are composed by Pratardana, who is clearly described as *Kasiraja* (king of Kashi). Kashi (Varanasi), as we know, lies in south-eastern Uttar Pradesh. The Puranas not only confirm that Pratardana was king of Kashi but name at least six of his predecessors.

One entire book (Book III), of the ten books of the Rigveda, is similarly authored by composers belonging to the family of Visvamitra. According to the Puranas, Visvamitra was the ninth descendant of Jahnu, who established the kingdom of Kanyakubja (Kanauj) in Uttar Pradesh. In the Rigveda the composer of the hymn refers to himself as belonging to the "house of Jahnu". In other words, the kingdom of Kanyakubja was in existence at least nine generations before the composition of any of the hymns in this book.

In two other hymns (VIII. 2.41) and (VII. 3. 21-24) the poet Kanva Medhatithi praises king Vibhindu and king Pakasthaman for their gifts and the Brahaddevata (VI. 42) clearly identifies them as rulers of Kashi and Bhoja (in eastern Uttar Pradesh and western Madhya Pradesh, respectively).

Another hymn (III. 53.14) mentions Kikata and its king Pramaganda. Kikata later came to be named Magadha. Thus south Bihar is also mentioned in the Rigveda.

This, however, raises the question whether the language of these hymns attributed to authors in present-day Uttar Pradesh, Madhya Pradesh and Bihar is different from other hymns composed in Punjab and, if so, how significant is the difference? Telageri has not posed this question.

That apart, however, the eastern Aryan theory provides us a possible explanation for the rise of non-Vedic Jainism and Buddhism. Both provide for 23 predecessors of the historically known founders – Mahavir and Gautam Buddha in the sixth century B.C. It may also help fill the gaps in our knowledge of the linguistic history of India, to which Suniti Kumar Chatterjee has drawn our attention. (See Chapter 2.)

According to Telageri the Vedic dialects disappeared in course of time and their speech area (Punjab and its environs) was taken over by the Inner-Indo-European dialects. But long before that, they had set in motion a cult movement which covered the entire country. This Vedic cult finally also gave way but continued to remain in force as the elite layer of a pan-Indian religion of the Inner-Indo-Europeans and Dravidians. Vedic hymns still dominate Hindu rituals but have little impact on the lives of Hindus.

Classical Sanskrit was created by ancient grammarians (Panini was preceded by hundreds of others, many of whom are named by him in his *Astadhyayi*) to serve as a via media between the Vedic language and the Inner-Indo-European dialects which had developed together with the Dravidian languages over the course of millennia and were therefore structurally different from the Vedic, and also had their own roots and words. Later the Prakrits came into vogue. Finally, the Inner dialects came into their own in the form of the new Indo-Aryan languages, as heavily Sanskritized as the Dravidian languages. India's cultural history thus begins with a grand synthesis.

Telageri's summing up is important. He says: "In short, the linguistic structure of the present Indo-Aryan languages is not a 'change' from an originally Vedic-like linguistic structure; it is a linguistic structure which developed, in the course of millennia, in the Inner-Indo-European speech family, in conjunction with the Dravidian languages."

I am not a specialist in this field. But as an interested student, I can say that it answers many of the problems philologists have faced and raised for around 200 years. It also settles the question of the cultural unity of India. The Aryans and the Dravidians together shaped the languages and culture of India.

Many other peoples named in the Rigveda are associated by other ancient Indian texts with other parts of India. In one hymn (VIII. 5. 3739), for example, we find a reference to the Cedis and their king Kasu. The Puranas point out that the Cedis were Yadavas who migrated northwards to Bundelkhand from Vidarbha in northern Maharashtra.

The poetess-composer of one Vedic hymn (1.179), Lopamudra, wife of Agastya, the great rishi known to be father of the Tamil grammar, is declared by every single ancient Indian text to be the daughter of the king of Vidarbha. Thus there were Aryan speakers in northern Maharashtra well before the composition of these hymns.

All in all, the Rigvedic hymns, in combination with the other texts show that the Indo-European language-speaking people of the time were not restricted to the Punjab region, but were found as far east as south Bihar and the Bay of Bengal, and as far south as Maharashtra. This is, more or less, the geographical extent of the Indo-Aryan languages to this day.

Some points may be made at this stage. The Vedas testify to the existence of the Purana in the Vedic period itself which obviously got divided into 18 and in the process expanded. These Puranas provide a genealogy of kings of major dynasties up to the time of the Mahabharata war. Telageri uses the list of about 100 kings provided by P. L. Bhargava.

On the basis of the excavation work by marine archaeologists belonging to the National Institute of Oceanography under the direction of Dr. S.R. Rao, the date of the submergence of Krishna's city of Dwarka can be fixed around 1500-1400 B.C., which, incidentally is also suggested by Puranic records which place it 1000 years before Nanda who ruled in Patliputra around 400 B.C.

Take the average reign of a king to be 18 years which is generally accepted by scholars. This takes us back to 3200-3100 B.C. The Aryans are supposed to have come into north-west India around 1500 B.C. and the Rigveda is dated 1000 B.C. at the earliest!

The 'conquering' Aryans are alleged to have treated the 'conquered' original inhabitants of India with contempt. The two words which have been used most to make to this charge stick are *Dasa* and *Dasyu*. The Rigveda throughout refers to *Dasa/Dasyus* as *asraddha* (faithless), *ayajna* (offering-less) and *avrata* (without rituals). It is obvious that these terms refer to religious practices, and not to race or language. As such they could apply only to would-be Iranians, who were hostile to the cult of Indra and to the sacrifice of animals in the sacred fire. This is not a matter of conjecture. Telageri shows that the Iranians called themselves by these names. The world *Dasyu* is found in the Avesta as *Dahya*, 's' becoming 'h' as in all Persian dialects. The word *Dasa* is found in the eastern Iranian dialect of Khotanese as *Daha* meaning 'man'. But some how the charge has stood.

The Rigveda makes it clear that *Dasa* and *Dasyu* are one and the same and so are *Dasyus* and *Asuras* in the later hymns when *Asura* has ceased to be the equal of *Devas* and come to acquire an unsavoury connotation.

Telageri is, therefore, justified in concluding that the *Arya-Dasyu* conflict in the Rigveda reflects the Vedic-versus Iranian conflict which took place in the Punjab region. After the bulk of the 'Iranians' left Punjab and migrated westwards, the terms *Dasa/Dasyu* ceased to be used in reference to a community, and came to be used only in the sense of 'slave' and 'robber', respectively.

Ten dynasties or peoples are mentioned in the Puranas; of them four are described in some detail. These are the Saryatis, Pramsus, Iksvakus (Ram belonged to this dynasty) and the Sudyumnas. The Sudyumnas are then divided into Drahyus, Anus, Turvasus, Yadus and Purus. Of them, the Anus, who lived close to the Purus in Kashmir, later became Iranians. This is confirmed by most ancient Iranian texts.

The first chapter of Vendidad lists 16 holy lands rendered unfit for man by Angra Manyu, the evil spirit of Zend Avesta. The first of these is Airyano Vaejo, bitterly cold and full of snow. If there is doubt that this refers to Kashmir, the designation of the next as Hapta Hindu, that is Sapta-Sindhu (Punjab) should remove it.

Since Punjab now contains five and not seven rivers, it may be added that the Saraswati, biggest of them in Vedic times, dried up about the same time as the so-called Indus Valley civilization disappeared around 1800 B.C., and another river Drishadvati, now known as Naiwala, is going dry.

Students of the Rigveda are familiar with the "battle of ten kings". The relevant hymns have been variously interpreted. Most of these interpretations cannot stand scrutiny. The details, however, do not concern us. Pertinent for us is the fact that the names mentioned there help us identify various Iranian peoples.

The Prthus are obviously Parthians of latter-day Iran, the Parsus the Persians, the Pakthas the Pakhtoons or the Pathans, the Bhalanas the Baluchis (witness Bolan pass), the Visanins Pisaca (Dardic people), and the Bhrgus ancestors of the Phyrgians.

As Telageri has put it, the evidence is overwhelming that eight groups of Anus mentioned in the Rigveda and the Puranas (seven of those being from the ten peoples named in a single historical incident) are the ancient and modern Iranian peoples, covering practically all the major ones: the Medes, the Persians, the Parthians, the Phrygians, the Khivs, the Dards (Pisacas), the Baluchis and the Pakhtoons. These peoples are today found stretched out westwards from Kashmir right up to Asia Minor.

Dr. S.R. Rao, the well-known archaeologist, has provided a valuable 'Foreword' which powerfully reinforces Telageri's case on the strength of archaeological evidence. Dr. Rao himself is a linguist of no mean achievement. Indeed, he has deciphered the script of the Indus Valley seals. This has begun to win wide, though not yet universal, recognition among scholars. Though the non-discovery so far of a bilingual seal remains a handicap, Dr. Rao's work is convincing in that it links the seals with a concrete (Vedic) culture, while others have speculated about a Dravidian culture which they have not defined.

Islam and the Nation Concept

S ome Muslim scholars have questioned the validity of the concept of Islamic state as distinct from Muslim state, the first being an ideological proposition which has never materialized in Muslim history because no Muslim state has ever been theocratic and the second being a fact of history in the past 1400 years. It would be recalled that the possibility and desirability of an Islamic state, that is, a state based on the Koran and the Hadith, had become a major issue of world-wide debate in view of the triumph of the mullah-led revolution in Iran in 1979.

These scholars have collected enormous historical evidence to establish the following points: that no Muslim state has ever been a theocracy in the proper sense of the term; that a power struggle began in Muslim society soon after the death of the Prophet; that of the four "rightly guided" caliphs, three died violent deaths; and that with the emergence of Muawiya as the caliph after the death of Ali, son-in-law of the Prophet, the concept of hereditary kingship triumphed; that this reality was not superseded in Muslim history till recently, and that the Islamic revolution in Iran in 1979 represents the first serious attempt even in Shia Islam to establish what can be called a theocracy.

In terms of facts, all this is irrefutable. The power struggle in the Muslim world has been as violent and unprincipled as anywhere else in the world; Muslim rulers have as a rule been as pleasure-loving and self-seeking as their counterparts elsewhere. But these facts need to be placed in what I for one regard as the proper perspective. This cannot be done unless we grasp the central point that Islamic society, as Gai Eaton has put it in his *Islam and the Destiny of Man*[1] is *theocentric* and not *theocratic*. The distinction is important and it is truly extraordinary that it has been missed in most of the writings on Islam.

The centrality of the state in human affairs is a modern development. Traditional societies regarded the state as no more than a necessary evil since large societies could no longer be managed on the old tribal basis. In the case of the Hindus, this proposition is widely accepted despite the theories modern apologists have propagated in the past one century. It is generally accepted that as a self-regulating community, the Hindus have not been unduly dependent on the state and indeed that they have managed to preserve their identity under prolonged foreign rule on that strength.

In the case of the Muslims, this reality has somehow got obscured perhaps partly because Muslim commentators have been keen to contrast their community with the Hindus and establish some kind of parity with the West just as they have been anxious to do the same on the issue of the "people of the book" in disregard of other explicit statements in the Koran itself and the entire Sufi tradition which is without question rooted in the Koran. The source of the confusion, of course, lies in Western scholarship which has sought to locate Islam in history and thus deny it its transcendental aspect which surely is the heart of Islam as it is of every religion. These questions are, however, too large to be discussed here.

To return to the question of the distinction between theocentrism and theocracy, it should hardly be necessary to define theocentrism. But it has become necessary to do so in view of the confusion that prevails. So it needs to be emphasized that for the Muslims, all sovereignty vests in God and that, indeed, nothing whatever exists or can exist outside of Him. It follows that God is the sole legislator; to quote Gai Eaton again, the Koranic insistence that "there is no god but God" can be interpreted to mean that "there is no legislator but the Legislator". That is precisely why for the Muslims their laws have to be derived from the Koran and the Sunnah of the Prophet. And they have been so derived in the past 14 centuries. And that is what has given the *ummah* the unity it has possessed despite all the political turmoils it has passed through. That would also explain why jurisprudence and not theology has been the main preoccupation of Islamic scholarship.

In such a scheme, the role of the ruler, good, bad or indifferent, must be strictly limited. Unlike pre-Islamic Egyptian kings, for example, he cannot claim to be viceregant of God on earth (incidentally in Islam all men are viceregents of God on earth in that 'man has been made in the image of God'); he cannot supersede the Shariat though changes have been made in it by some Muslim rulers in recent years; he can manipulate the ulema and make them issue *fatwas* in his favour but that only establishes the point that he is not a priest-king. And how can there be a theocracy without a priest-king? Indeed, 'secular' communist rulers have been more like priest-kings than Muslim rulers.

Two other points need to be made in this regard. First, the Prophet, who spoke in great detail on a great number of issues, had little to say on government as such; he showed no interest in theorizing on politics. And there is a tradition which speaks for itself. One of his companions is said to have requested him that he be appointed governor of one of the recently conquered territories. "No," said the Prophet, "if you wish to rule, then you are unfit." According to another tradition recorded by both Bukhari and Muslim, the Prophet said: "Do not ask for rulership, for if you are given power as a result of asking for it, you will be left to deal with it on your own, if you are given it without asking, then you will be helped in exercising it." It should not be necessary to add that hardly has any Muslim ruler ever lived up to the Prophet's prescription.

Second, it was years after the death of the Prophet that the theory of leadership (caliphate) was worked out by Muslim jurists, and under this theory, it has been clearly understood that the prophetic function had ended with the death of Mohammed and that his successors inherited only the political function and the duty of administering the laws set out in the Koran and the Prophet's sayings and practices. The caliph had three functions. He was the viceregent of the Prophet as temporal head of the *ummah*; he was the imam of the community and upholder of the law; and finally, he was commander of the faithful for the defence and expansion of Islam.

The central issue in Islam has not been whether the state can be separated from religion but whether society can be separated from religion. It is because the answer to the second has to be firmly in the negative that the answer to the first has also to be in the negative. In posing the first question – whether the state can be separated from religion – without simultaneously posing the second – whether society can be separated from religion – scholars have, to use the old cliché, sought to put the cart before the horse.

The modern mind just cannot comprehend Islam precisely because it is a totality. Islamic society is rooted in the religion of Islam; it is not the other way about. The point needs to be heavily underscored that Islamic society is wholly unlike Christian society in terms of which it is judged. Unlike Mohammed, Christ did not give his people the law; Christians inherited the Roman law; in plain terms, Christianity did not represent a break from the Graeco-Roman past except in the field of religion narrowly defined. Islamic law is not rooted in pre-Islamic Arab traditions; it is rooted in the Koran and the Sunnah of the Prophet. As such Islamic society was a new "creation" even if old materials had gone into its making in the sense Christian society was not a new "creation." *Sanatan Dharma*, which is now called Hinduism, is a similar totality. But that is another issue which I cannot even touch upon here.

As Islam stepped out of the spartan Arab setting in its formative period, its rulers were bound to succumb to the ways of the Byzantinian and the Sassanid empires they inherited, and they so succumbed. The glorious Muslim civilization that we admire and the Muslims take great pride in was, however, in no small measure the product of this development.

One aspect of this great civilization has not attracted the attention which, in my view, it deserves. It created a divide between the Persianized sophisticated and pleasure-loving upper crust and the pious and the ordinary Muslims, a rift which has not healed despite Islam's insistence on equality. This rift could have proved fatal for Islam, especially in the context of the introduction of the Aristotlean rationalist "poison" into Islamic philosophy, if the state had acquired the kind of power it now enjoys in society. Islamic society has survived because over much of its history the state has been so marginal to it.

The gulf between Islamic exoterism as represented by the ulema and Islamic esoterism as represented by the Sufis of different orders is too wide to be glossed over. The great Ghazzali sought to reconcile the two but his success

could in the nature of things be only limited. But the fact
stands out that the two together have ensured the
survival of Islam. Without the ulema, Islam could not
have protected its external defences and without the
Sufis, Islam would have lacked the capacity for self-
renewal and been reduced to a mausoleum. There is an
inner dialectic in Islam, which the modern man,
indoctrinated by the West, is unable to see.

As Islam expanded, beginning with the time of the
Prophet, it could not possibly be ruled from one centre.
The surprise, if any, is that the institution of the caliphate
survived till the second decade of this century even if in
a shadowy form. Temporal authority had to fragment.
Empires and kingdoms had to arise. These divisions had
to be based partly on the fact of conquest and partly on
ethnicity and geography. But Muslim states territorially
defined as we know them today are the imperialist West's
handiwork. Having come into existence, though as a
result of accidents of history, they are likely to stay on
more or less in their present boundaries. But they cannot
by virtue of their existence become nation-states, unless
it is assumed that Islam will be reduced to the status of
a small compartment in the totality of society as
Christianity has been in the West.

The nation concept is the product of developments
over centuries in Europe. It does not represent only the
triumph of the province over the priest; it represents the
triumph of an altogether new approach to life. Along with
its twin brother, secularism, it represents the triumph of
matter over spirit and of reason over intellect which the
Hindus call *buddhi*. The contrast between the traditional
(religious) and the modern approach is best illustrated by
the difference in their concept of the origin of man. The
Manu of the Hindus and the Adam of the Christians and
the Muslims was a semi-divine figure. Manu being the
original law-giver and Adam in Islam the first Prophet
and in Christianity the perfect man who allowed himself

to be beguiled; the modern West traces our ancestry to
the ape.

The nation is a new god (nothing short of it) which
feels entitled to demand, and has succeeded in extracting,
from the people the kind of sacrifices no religion has ever
demanded; millions upon millions have been killed and
maimed in the name of the nation god. This god could
not have arisen without the help of its twin brother,
secularism. Indeed, they are like Siamese twins who
cannot be separated. A nation must by definition be
secular because it can rise only on the corpse of religion;
a secular state is a logical extension of a secular nation.
To be secular is not to be necessarily intolerant of religion.
Communism is an unnecessarily ugly face of secularism
just as it is an unnecessarily crude face of the modern
Western civilization as such, that is gross materialism
unrelieved by the residue of Christainity in the shape of
humanism. Again, philosophic materialism must not be
confused with 'this-worldliness'. This-worldliness without
the philosophic underpinning is defensive; it seeks to
cover itself behind some façade. Philosophic materialism
(secularism) is self-confident and aggressive. Powerful
battalions are ranged behind it in the form of modern
scientists, technologists and what not.

This story began with the Renaissance, if not much
earlier, with St. Thomas Aquinas (who replaced Platonic
categories with Aristotlean ones and thus exposed Christianity to split and erosion from within), proceeded via the
Reformation when the so-called individual conscience
came to be accorded primacy over the collectivity, and got
consummated in the French Revolution, preceded and
followed by debunking of all tradition, glorification of the
individual, of change, of material comfort, of speed and
the whole rigmarole called modernism. Neither the nation
concept nor the secularism concept stands by itself. Both
are integral parts of a complex framework of which
religion, any religion, can constitute only a marginal
component.

The Old Order Changeth...

The socio-economic-political order Jawaharlal Nehru fashioned and Indira Gandhi and Rajiv Gandhi kept going, with modifications, is in deep trouble. It cannot possibly be restored to health. The changes that have been launched in the economy, beginning with devaluation of the rupee by around 20 per cent, cannot help rescue the old order. If they are allowed to proceed by the logic of their inner dynamism which is doubtful, they must instead transform the system and produce a new one. A comparison with the former Soviet Union, or former Soviet satellites, will clearly be overdrawn. But, in some ways, the comparison may not be wholly inept. The Nehru order, after all, was a product of the cold war.

An intricate power arrangement has informed the economic order which is now sought to be reshaped. The power holders and power brokers are too numerous and too well entrenched at all levels of Indian public life and administration to be quickly and painlessly dislodged. They will fight back. The stakes are high. The minister of state for commerce boasted after the announcement of the new import-export policy in early July 1991 that he was told that he had given away around Rs. 70 crores a year by way of bribes for himself!

Nehru's personality, as has been discussed all too often, was doubtless an important factor in his choice of the 'socialist' path to industrialization, with its emphasis on the primacy of the public and the subordination of the private sector. So was the fact of the availability of Soviet assistance for heavy and basic industries. But Nehru could not have carried the day in the ruling Congress party, generally inclined to be anti-communist, if he had not enjoyed the backing of a powerful constituency virtually in a position to clinch the issue.

Nehru's was basically the same constituency – the intelligentsia – which had brought about the communist revolution in Russia. Incidentally, that would explain support and sympathy for the Soviet 'experiment' in India, despite the exposure of its inhuman face and the existence of Gulag archipelago, and much else, indeed the Nehruvian framework and the survival in good odour of the two communist parties even after the collapse of communist regimes in Europe and the outbreak of a crisis of unknown proportions in the Soviet Union.

The Indian intelligentsia was too big and heterogeneous even at the time of independence in 1947 to be treated as a radical monolith. It was nothing of the kind. The degree of alienation of Western educated men and women from their own traditions varied greatly and so did their commitment to the cause of revolution, of which freedom from British rule was only one, though the most important aspect. An overwhelming majority of them, however, shared a number of features.

They mostly came from modest non-business, indeed anti-business, backgrounds, the priestly Brahmin one being the most important. They could regard themselves as members of the 'middle class', largely on the strength of their educational qualifications and entitlement to white collar jobs. Their first search was for security of employment with the government which also happened to be the only truly big employer of educated Indians.

Nehru was their idol from the time of his rise to prominence in the Indian National Congress, the party of the freedom movement, in the twenties, precisely because he was the most Westernized of Congress leaders as well as the most critical of the pillars of the pre-British, as well as of the British, order – the landed gentry and the business class. Mahatma Gandhi too swept this class of Indians off their feet. But Indian intellectuals gave him at best a grudging acceptance. They regarded him as being antediluvian in social and economic matters.

There was doubtless a gap between members of the intelligentsia who joined the government in some capacity and those who took to agitation against the British, in the first instance, primarily because the imperial order could not create enough jobs for them and refused to concede social equality to them which they were convinced was their due by virtue of their Western education. Indianization of the services and admission to British clubs were, it may be recalled, among the earliest demands of Indian nationalists.

The gap between the two groups, however was not so wide as not to be partly bridged. While, for instance, Jawaharlal's father, Motilal Nehru, joined the freedom movement under Mahatma Gandhi's leadership, his first cousins used their considerable influence to secure entry into the elite Indian Civil Service – the famous steel frame of the empire – for their sons. Both were to hold important positions under Nehru as prime minister.

As independent India's first home minister, Sardar Vallabhbhai Patel recognized the need to reassure the bureaucracy and to win its willing cooperation for the consolidation of India's freedom. He took steps to do both. Nehru, as was his wont, continued to castigate the bureaucracy for its unresponsiveness to popular aspirations and needs. But he did something for it which neither the Sardar nor any Congress leader we know of would have done. In the name of development, equity and prevention of accumulation of too much wealth in the hands of a few business houses, he placed the economy under its control and therefore at its disposal.

Bureaucrats were not slow to take advantage of the unprecedented opportunity that had unexpectedly come their way. They created a web of controls and regulations of Byzantine complexity, through which they alone could help desperate businessmen find their way, of course, for a fee. In course of time, India's became one of the most regulated economies outside the communist world, and thereby one of the most corrupt polities and bureaucracies.

Socialism, a euphemism for an economy dominated by bureaucrats and politicians, was the central pillar of the Nehru system and that essentially remained the case, under Indira Gandhi and Rajiv Gandhi. Indira Gandhi began to recognize the need to liberalize controls and regulations on her return to office in January 1980. She, however, was too conscious of her popular appeal based on reckless populism in the past, and too cautious in her approach to liberate the economy of the political-bureaucratic stranglehold in a significant way.

Rajiv Gandhi appeared to adopt a bolder approach when he took over as Prime Minister on the assassination of his mother in October 1984. But he too found it necessary to accompany the programme of easing controls by punitive raids on leading business houses as if to keep them terrorized and aware of their lowly place in the Indian power hierarchy. He chose in V.P. Singh a finance minister who positively revelled in ordering such raids and regarded raids as a passport to political prominence which he had not enjoyed earlier. His calculations proved to be right. That is one index of India's anti-business political culture.

As is well known, non-alignment in the East-West conflict, with a clear tilt in favour of the Soviet Union, and secularism, never coherently and meaningfully defined by anyone in authority, have been the other two pillars of the Nehru-Indira-Rajiv order. Obviously, non-alignment is over with the collapse of the Soviet bloc, however unwilling its proponents may be to recognize this reality, even after the ridiculous stance it pushed them into at the time of the war against Iraq by the US-led coalition for the liberation of Kuwait and the destruction of the awesome military machine Saddam Hussain had assembled. Thus apparently only one of the three pillars – secularism – can be said to be still in place. Surely, one pillar cannot support a structure so far sustained by three. But before I deal with the new situation, it would be in order to examine the leadership and the support-base system of the Congress.

Mahatma Gandhi introduced in the Congress a style of leadership – leadership from above – which has characterized the party ever since, however stark the differences between the personalities of the leaders – between the Mahatma and Nehru, between Nehru and Indira Gandhi between Indira Gandhi and Rajiv Gandhi. The Mahatma did not rise in the party hierarchy. He, in a manner of speaking, descended on it from above, having made his name and perfected his techniques in South Africa. He just took over the organization, such as it was, after the First World War and remained its supreme leader till his assassination on 30 January 1948. He resigned as an ordinary member of the Congress as if to make the point that his leadership was not contingent on such 'formalities'.

Jawaharlal Nehru too came into the Congress leadership from 'above'. He did not graduate into it, as did others. Indira Gandhi had, in a sense, to struggle for supremacy in the party but only after the top position had been conceded to her in the first instance. Her conflict with the organizational bosses began after they had placed her in the powerful office of Prime Minister. She vanquished them first in 1969 and then in 1978 and converted the Congress into a praetorian guard for the family. That is why it came to be, and continues to be, described as Congress (Indira). The dynasty had been consolidated. Rajiv Gandhi succeeded her without the slightest resistance in a true dynastic style. His leadership was not questioned even after a series of electoral defeats, culminating in the loss of power for the party at the Centre in 1989.

All this is recalled to make two points. First, the Congress has had no experience of doing without a supreme leader. As such, it cannot be easy for it to make the transition to what, in the communist jargon popular in India, has come to be known as collective leadership. The psychology of dependence explains the pressure on Sonia Gandhi to assume leadership of the party, her lack of experience, well-advertised distaste for politics and her Italian origins notwithstanding. The party will be in trouble whether she heeds, or does not heed, the call.

Secondly, the primacy of the leadership principle in the Congress has been an important factor in assuring for it the support of the minorities and the weakest sections of the Hindu society. For, only a leader in a position to place himself or herself above the organization can be attractive to them because the organization must otherwise mirror intra-Hindu conflicts as well as broad Hindu aspirations.

In the wake of the partition of India, which accompanied independence in 1947, Nehru was the only Congress leader who could have won the loyalty of Muslims. Just as he was the only prominent socialist left in the organization after Congress socialists had quit the organization en masse in 1948 to form their own party, and the only neutralist in the East-West struggle, he was also the only 'secularist' in the topmost Congress leadership. Thus as far as Muslims were concerned, he alone could have presided over the foundation of the kind of support base for the Congress which has helped it stay in power most of the time since independence.

The scheduled castes and tribes too trusted him more than they trusted any other Congress leader precisely because he was the most Westernized of them all and most insistent in his opposition to the Hindu social order which sanctioned untouchability. Among themselves, the scheduled castes (roughly 15 per cent), Muslims (12 per cent) and tribes (6 per cent) constitute one-third of India's population and are generally believed to have provided the Congress one-half of its total vote in most elections. Caste Hindus, accounting for two-thirds of the population, have supplied the other half.

Things did not change much under Indira Gandhi, except in 1977 when a majority of Muslims are estimated to have voted against the Congress because they were aggrieved on account of the slum clearance and family planning campaigns Sanjay Gandhi had conducted during the emergency (June 1975 to March 1977). As for Rajiv Gandhi, in 1989 Muslims voted against the Congress largely in protest against what they regard as its pro-Hindu bias on the temple-mosque dispute in Ayodhya (UP) and riots in various towns in Uttar Pradesh and Bihar.

Examined carefully in the context of the average Congress vote of around 44 per cent before 1989, one weakness of the Congress support base is obvious. It shows that while among the weaker sections of society, every two out of three who exercised their franchise voted for the Congress, only one out of three did so among caste Hindus who must, by any reckoning, be regarded as India's mainstream. They constitute the majority, they are far better educated, and they dominate in every sphere of activity except the crafts.

Another weakness would be equally obvious if we were to take note of the fact that there can be no unity of interest between the different constituents of the coalition, between Muslims and scheduled castes, for instance. The coalition was also unstable since any attempt by the Congress to widen its support base among Hindus, as under Indira Gandhi, tended to alienate Muslims and vice versa. To put it differently, the support base could hold and be effective best in the absence of a serious challenge and in conditions of stability. The period of stability ended with Nehru in 1964.

The Congress leadership was dominated by Brahmins during the freedom struggle just as was the bureaucracy by virtue of the same fact of Western education. This dominance came to be challenged in south India and western India soon after independence, partly because the Brahmin presence there was rather thin since Brahmins there were migrants from north India, and partly because an anti-Brahmin movement had prospered in the Madras presidency as well as the Bombay presidency under the Raj. In both these regions the party organization was effectively taken over by upcoming peasant (earlier warrior as well) communities by the mid-fifties. A similar change could not take place in north India and that has been its Achilles' heel there. North India accounts for around two-thirds of the electorate and representation in Parliament.

The Congress party suffered its first big reverse in north India in 1967 when it lost power in all states in the region from Himachal Pradesh in the north-west to West Bengal in the east. This was repeated on an even bigger scale in 1977 when the debacle led to the loss of power at the Centre itself for the first time since 1947. On both occasions, upcoming peasant communities, unable to seize control of the ruling party, unlike in south India and western India, played a key role in its rout. The communities are, however, notoriously fractious and unable to throw up leaders who can stay together, especially in victory. So they fell apart both times, making it possible for the Congress to stage a comeback under Indira Gandhi's leadership in 1969 and in 1980.

This was, however, a temporary recovery and the old story has been repeated in quick succession in the 1989 and 1991 polls. Though the defeat in 1989 has not been as devastating as in 1977, it has been particularly significant on another count. Almost all leading Brahmin candidates, including stalwarts such as the former Uttar Pradesh Chief Minister Narain Dutt Tiwari and the Bihar Chief Minister Jagannath Mishra have bitten dust in their own constituencies. The party is thus rendered leaderless in a fundamental sense.

The Congress, as noted earlier, has always had a large Brahmin presence in its top central leadership and even state leadership in much of north India. This presence was strengthened as a result of the 1967 general election when a number of non-Brahmin leaders such the party chief Kamaraj Nadar (Tamil Nadu), party treasurer S.K. Patil (Bombay), and Atulya Ghosh (party boss in West Bengal) were defeated, and then of the split in the Congress in 1969 when Indira Gandhi drove them out. Rajiv Gandhi maintained the status quo. Thus there is a dramatic break with the past. Suddenly, the character of the party has changed in two other significant ways. It has become predominantly a south Indian and western Indian party and it has no individual capable of providing charismatic leadership of the type it has been used to.

There is, on the face of it, an ephemeral quality about developments which have transformed the Indian political scene since 1987 when Rajiv Gandhi came under pressure on the Bofors payoff issue. Three of these deserve notice. One: V. P. Singh's exit in 1987 first from the government on the question of an inquiry he ordered as defence minister into the HDW submarine deal without the prior consent of Rajiv Gandhi, and then from the party on the issue of the appointment of the American company Fairfax to look into alleged violations of foreign exchange regulations by Indian corporations and individuals when he held the finance portfolio, again without the prior consent of the prime minister. Two: V.P. Singh's sudden decision as prime minister in August 1989 to order implementation of the Mandal Commission report favouring 22.5 per cent reservations in government and semi-government jobs for the so-called 'other backward castes', 'other' than the scheduled castes. Three: the response of L. K. Advani, leader of the avowedly Hindu organization, the Bharatiya Janata Party, to it.

It can well be argued that V. P. Singh could have ordered the inquiry in 1987 with Rajiv Gandhi's consent; that Rajiv Gandhi need not have regarded it as a frontal challenge to his authority; that V. P. Singh could have consulted Advani on the Mandal question since the survival of his minority government was critically dependent on the BJP's support from the outside and the BJP had committed itself to implementation of the report in its election manifesto; and that there was no good reason for him to rush this decision just because a rival peasant leader in his own party, Devi Lal, was holding a mass rally in New Delhi two days later.

On the question of the Mandal Commission report, it is difficult to be sure whether V.P. Singh acted out of panic in the face of a challenge by his former deputy prime minister, Devi Lal, or out of calculation that the rally gave him a pretext to silence dissent among his Cabinet colleagues and allies. Be that as it may, the ferocity of opposition to the decision among students, who in addition to resorting to methods of protest including attacking public property, usual in India, took to acts of self-immolation in their dozens, speaks as much of the potency of the fire V.P. Singh had stoked as does his lionization as the second Buddha by Mandal enthusiasts.

The question was not of social justice. It was of power. The 'other backward castes' were able to challenge the examination system of recruitment to government jobs because some of them, such as the Yadavs in Uttar Pradesh and Bihar, had done remarkably well economically and politically and sought to capture the state apparatus through reservations. They provided the numbers and muscle for V. P. Singh's ascent to the office of Prime Minister in 1989.

The Mandal decision was deeply divisive of Hindus in north India and potentially disruptive of the quality of the administration. No administration can cope with as high a level of reservations as 50 per cent: 27 per cent jobs in the government are already reserved for scheduled castes and tribes and certain categories and the Mandal Commission report provides for 22.5 per cent more reservations.

V.P. Singh could not have been unaware of this reality. Perhaps he did not care. Perhaps he made the move precisely because he knew it would greatly embarrass the BJP in view of its commitment to unite Hindus. Whatever his calculations and intentions, the BJP had to fight back and it could not do so on the ground of his choice. It had to look for another.

That, as it happened, lay ready in the shape of the temple-mosque dispute. Advani got into the chariot – a jeep shaped into the kind of chariot ancient Indian warriors are thought to have used. The popular response surpassed the wildest expectations of the BJP and allied organizations. Cornered by V.P. Singh's Mandal move and buoyed up with the popular response to the *rath yatra*, the BJP withdrew support and brought down the government.

Here again we are faced with one of those 'buts and ifs' of history. For we can only speculate on what the outcome of the election, rendered unavoidable by the fall of the government in November 1989, would have been if the ruling Janata Dal had not split and the breakaway faction allowed, with the support of the Congress, to form a new government with Chandra Shekhar as prime minister. But as events developed, three more or less evenly balanced formations entered the electoral arena in March 1991 – the Congress, the BJP and National Front-Left combine, with the Janata Dal as the principal component of the National Front in north India and regional parties in south India. Two of them have come out badly mauled – the Congress and the National Front.

The Congress has been decimated in Uttar Pradesh and Bihar. Gains elsewhere cannot compensate for this loss.

India is obviously passing through a period of great turbulence. As such, it is difficult to say that this is a period of transition and that India will, as in the past, soon achieve a measure of stability either as a result of the recovery of the Congress, or of a further expansion in the influence of the BJP. Indeed, it would not be prudent even to write off the Janata Dal under V. P. Singh's leadership, though in view of the experience of a similar assertion by the middle peasantry in the past, it would not be surprising if it turns out that the Dal has peaked its influence and is on the way down. All that can, in my assessment, be ruled out is the much talked about realignment of political forces and that too with the qualification that the Janata Dal might still split and the dissidents join the Congress.

That apart, the supposedly unlikely realignment of forces in opposition to the BJP is unlikely to materialize. Ever since the twenties when the Communist Party of India was established, communists and leftists sympath-

etic to the 'cause', have been expecting (read wanting) the
Congress to split into 'progressive' and 'reactionary' wings
and the 'progressive' factions to make common cause with
them. The Congress split in 1969 to their advantage, but
it turned out to be a temporary one; the game was up
with the imposition of emergency in 1975. It split again
in 1978, to no advantage to them. If it splits again which
appears unlikely, the gainer will, in all probability, be the
BJP.

Similarly, contrary to what is being said by several
commentators, it does not appear to me that India has
entered an era of coalitions Italian-style. A two-party
system has crystallized in most states. Except in Uttar
Pradesh where the BJP and the Janata Dal are the
principal contenders for power, in other states the
Congress is still either the ruling party or the main
opposition party. Unless this situation changes radically
to the disadvantage of the Congress, an alliance with it
at the Centre is not possible.

Equally pertinently, a careful reading of Indian history
will reveal an undying yearning for a strong Centre. In
practice this yearning was often not fulfilled before the
British arrived on the scene because the necessary
technical resources such as quick means of transport and
communication were not available. But the search never
ceased. The *Chakravartin* (universal ruler) ideal found
expression, even if a partial one, in one kingdom after
another right from the time of the Mauryas in fourth
century B.C. to the Mughal empire in the sixteenth and
seventeenth.

By this reckoning, India must possess an all-India
party, capable of providing firm government in New Delhi,
though India's diversity too must, by the same logic, find
greater expression than it has under the Congress
dispensation.

If my assessment of the Congress in respect of its ideological superstructure, leadership and support-base problems, as outlined earlier, is not too wide off the mark, the conclusion would be unavoidable that the BJP is the party of the future. That indeed appears to be the case to me.

The BJP is not a communal party: it cannot be, for the simple reason that Hindus have never been, and are not, a community in the accepted sense of the term. They represent an ancient civilization not known either to draw a boundary between the faithful and the faithless, the blessed and the damned, or to engage in heresy hunting and its counterpart, persecution of other faiths. Hindus are, in Western terms, pagans. Religion is a Semitic enterprise and is alien to their spirit and ways. They have no book and no church.

It is true that the BJP has helped the VHP arouse Hindus on the temple-mosque issue and that it owes much of its electoral success, both in 1989 and 1991, to this arousal. Since Muslim leaders have resisted its plea to agree to a shifting of the mosque to another site, though it has not been in use as a Muslim place of prayer and cannot be put back into use in view of the presence in it of Ram's idol since 1949, the campaign has acquired an anti-Muslim bias. But witness the fact that even the VHP has not laid claim to over 3000 sites which, on Muslim testimony itself, were once temples and are now mosques, and that the BJP has not supported the VHP's demand for even the two most important of them in the holy (for Hindus) cities of Banaras and Mathura.

But however one may regard this specific dispute in terms of its power and propriety, it is not the core issue. Which is whether the future of India is going to be shaped in some way in accordance with the spirit of Indian civilization which alone, of all old civilizations, is capable of self-renewal and self-affirmation because it alone has been able to maintain a living contact with its pre-historic past and to retain a measure of coherence by virtue of a faithful preservation and yet constant reinterpretation of the enormous corpus of ancient knowledge and practice.

This question was bypassed at the time of independence. Most Western-educated Indians are still not ready to grapple with it. That is why there is so much hostility among them to the BJP. But the 'Maginot line' has been breached. The BJP has broken through it. It may not be a mere coincidence that this has happened at the same time that communism has collapsed and the civilizational issue is beginning to surface in intra-European, Europe-US, Europe-Japan and Japan-US relations. There can, of course, be no return to the past in India as there cannot be in Japan and Europe. New perspectives can, however, develop. Unlike Islamic fundamentalists, the BJP does not claim to possess a blueprint. It shall have to struggle to evolve an Indian approach to modern problems.

Combining Bhakti with Power

Some liberal Hindus and Muslims have been highly critical of what I have written on the demolition of the Babri structure and related issues since 6 December 1992. They expect me to define my position on the question of the place of Muslims in India. Even if I ignore the implicit insinuation (and in some cases explicit) in it, the suggestion is misplaced. I see myself as an analyst of developments and not as a grand architect, or an ideologue, of an ideal India. Indeed, I distrust ideologies and ideologues. My main difficulty, however, is with the idiom in which the public discourse has been conducted in our country for over seven decades, that is, since the ascendancy of the Gandhi-Nehru leadership in the freedom movement. I would describe it as the liberal-Marxist-Gandhian idiom. Pandit Nehru has been the foremost expression and user of this idiom and conti- nues to dominate our discourse even in death.

This proposition must come as a surprise to most readers. For, Pandit Nehru has generally been regarded as a liberal and a Marxist and not as a Gandhian. Indeed, the popular perception of him is that he was opposed to the Gandhian approach. There is some merit in this view as far as issues like the place of village industry *vis-à-vis* large industry is concerned. But there was a deeper identity of approach between the two leaders which explains why Gandhiji designated Pandit Nehru as his successor.

Western thinkers had merged liberalism and Marxism to produce the theory of democratic socialism and in the process emasculated both. It was in fashion under the title of Fabianism in Britain when Pandit Nehru was a young student there. He just picked it up.

Nehru did not have to struggle too hard to accommodate Gandhism in his democratic socialism either. Even when he was alive, Gandhiji's own close lieutenants had divested Gandhian thought and practice of dynamism resulting from the Mahatma's own immersion in *Sanatan Dharma* and reduced it to a programme of social action and reform. So diminished it could not have escaped being subsumed by the powerful liberal-Marxist thought current which claimed to address the same questions of social reforms and justice.

In terms of will power, Gandhiji was doubtless one of the finest examples India has ever produced. But there is no evidence to show that he grasped the need for, and logic of, state power. Not to speak of his critics, he saw himself as a Ram *bhakt*. But, he was a *bhakt* not of Ram in his totality, that is of Ram the warrior also, but of Ram as *Purushottam Purusha*, that is, of Ram who set the ideal for ethical life.

This aspect of Gandhiji's personality and of the idiom he used and popularized has been ignored. As a result, it is generally not realized that *bhakti* uninterested in the power dimension of life has informed the thinking of educated Indians for centuries.

As one of many constituents of Indian spirituality before Muslim invasions and rule, *bhakti* was one proposition; it was then accompanied by other spiritual currents as well as an extensive search for, and exercise of, state power. As a dominant current under Muslim rule, more often than not extremely harsh and debilitating, it assumed an altogether different significance. It doubtless helped protect Hindu culture in extremely difficult circumstances, even if in an emasculated and rigid form. But it also promoted escapism as a way of life.

This is well illustrated by the fact that the crippling 'ideals' of poverty, austerity, indifference to social reality and power came to be widely cherished. The Bhakti movement became both an expression and an instrument of fragmentation of the Hindu vision and personality. As a result excessive emphasis came to be placed on certain aspects earlier meant not for householders but for renouncers and ascetics.

Muslim power did not sit easily on rural India. No Muslim ruler even acquired the capacity either to disarm the peasantry or destroy local leaders. And vast and thick forests provided excellent terrain for guerilla warfare. The British Raj managed to disarm the peasantry, destroy large forests, and make the local leaders dependent on it for their very survival. The *bhakti* psychology was thus powerfully reinforced.

This psychology explains the easy acceptance by the urban Hindu elite of the alien concepts of liberalism and Marxism. As noted earlier, their merger to constitute the theory of democratic socialism involved the emasculation of both. Since this is not a familiar proposition, some additional observations would be in order.

No serious student of history of ideas in the West will deny that liberalism is anti-power and anti-state in its origins and essence. Its concern is the mythical individual torn out of the social fabric. While it could, in the name of that nonexistent individual, help 'legitimize' private greed and economic growth as an offshot of that greed, socialism of whatever variety must inevitably deny it that role.

Socialism too is anti-state in its origins and essence. It is a child of Utopianism and a twin brother of anarchism which liberalism as the philosophic foundation of capitalism must, in its turn, seek to frustrate. The Marxist concept of dictatorship of the proletariat would have remained the meaningless prattle it was if Lenin had not conceived of and built an army of professional revolutionaries and subordinated that army called the Communist Party to his will. This was a case of total inversion of the original idea. That kind of concentration of power is negation of power and not its fulfilment.

Indian intellectual life has not overcome this troublesome legacy more than 45 years after the achievement of independence and the 'exercise' of state power in fulfilment of responsibilities that must devolve on rulers of a country. The magnitude of corruption, a euphemism for abuse of public authority and resources for personal ends from top to bottom of the state machinery, is one consequence of that legacy. Other more readily intelligible illustrations belong to the field of foreign policy and defence.

Only a leader lacking in sense of history and recognition of the logic of power could ridicule the twin theories of power vacuum and balance of power and only an elite similarly handicapped could endorse him. Similarly, only a political leadership contemptuous of Kshatriya values could keep out service chiefs from the formulation of the country's defence policy and its implementation. It is just inconceivable that our chiefs would be able to exercise the kind of influence General Collin Powell has been seen to do in respect of the Gulf war and the deployment of US forces in Somalia. He determined the level of force and equipment he would require before he would act and President George Bush complied.

Right or wrong, this is my view of the idiom of the Indian public discourse and should help make intelligible my rejection of it. This would also explain my difficulty in discussing the Muslim problem in a manner which is accessible to my readers. Meanwhile, if I have acted as an iconoclast, it is only because it cannot be helped if the deck is to be cleared for a meaningful debate.

Notes and References

Chapter 1

1. The Muslim kings were never able to consolidate their hold over India. Even the Mughal empire, at the height of its power, was plagued by what J.C. Heesterman has called the "inner frontier", i.e., the frontier beyond which its hold was tenuous. Indeed, the Mughal rulers, too, functioned essentially as "superzamindars" and remained critically dependent on the support of local nobles.
2. This translation has been brought out by Aditya Prakashan, New Delhi, 1991.
3. Dirk H.A. Kolff, *Naukar, Rajput and Sepoy*, Cambridge University Press, London, 1990.
4. Muslim rule, however we may define it, did not bring about a significant change in the economic order. The same old castes, for instance, continued to serve as rent collectors and dominate the country's commerce and trade. Thus, by and large, economic power, remained with the same groups. This is best illustrated by the fact that, during his struggle for power, Aurangzeb borrowed Rs. 4 lakh from a Hindu banker in Ahmedabad, and, at the time of the British takeover of Bengal in the eighteenth century, a vast majority of rent collectors were non-Muslim. That is how they became the principal beneficiaries of the Permanent Settlement.

Chapter 2

1. René Guenon, *Introduction to the Study of the Hindu Doctrines*, Luzac & Co., London, 1945, p. 105.

2. *Ibid.*, pp. 90-91.

3. Sri Aurobindo, *On the Vedas*, Sri Aurobindo Ashram, Pondicherry, 1964, p. 38.

4. M.G. Gupta, *Mystic Symbolism in Ramayana, Mahabharata and Pilgrim's Progress*, M.G. Publishers, Agra, 1993.

5. There cannot be the slightest doubt that since the Vedas, South Asia has been covered by a civilization, of which, these are the most eloquent, earliest surviving expression. Indian culture cannot be said to be rooted in anything other than the Vedas, not only because nothing older survives, but also because nothing basically alien to them can be located in any part of the land.

6. A number of scholars also have come to reject the Aryan invasion/migration theory and also to question the Aryan-Dravidian divide. Some of them have put back the date of the Rig Veda to the tenth millennium B.C. instead of the standard second. In this context, the well-known archaeologist, Dr. S.R. Rao, has established fairly conclusively that the so-called Indus Valley civilization was Vedic and not pre-Vedic and that it covered at least 1.5 million sq. km of territory. This new 'turn of events' has an important bearing on our understanding of the history of Iran as well and, consequently, of Indian Islam, because Islam as a civilization came to us via Iran and through the medium of the Persian language and Persian or Persianized poets, Sufis and others.

7. Stuart H. Blackburn and A.K. Ramanujan (eds.), *Another Harmony: New Essays on the Folklore of India*, Oxford University Press, New Delhi, 1986, p. 14.

8. Anncharlott Eschmann, Hermann Kulke and Gaya Charan Tripathi (eds.), *The Cult of Jagannath and the Regional Tradition of Orissa*, Manohar Books, New Delhi, 1986, p. xv.

9. *Ibid.*, p. 85.

10. *Ibid.*, p. 93.

11. *Ibid.*, p. 97.

12. *Ibid.*

13. Louis Dumont, *Homo Hierarchicus*, Paladin, London, 1970.

14. *Ibid.*, p. 194.

15. Some 2000 years ago, the ancient Tamils began to employ, from their own language, the word *Ar'am* as an equivalent of *Dharma* in Sanskrit. This word meant 'virtue in general'. Indeed, *Dharma* itself would appear to be connected with an old Tamil world, *ar'a*, which means 'path' or 'way'. The concept of *Dharma* is fundamental to Indian civilization as *Tao* and *Yeh* to the Chinese and *Logos* and *Nous* to the Greek. The Mahabharata, considered to be one of India's greatest literary works, is replete with the

Dharma concept. Both Buddhism and Jainism fall within the orbit of *Dharma*. The word *Arya* was added to *Dharma*, when it came to be interpreted in non-ethnic terms to mean 'noble' or 'superior'. See *India: A Polyglot Nation and its Linguistic Problems vis-à-vis National Integration*, Mahatma Gandhi Memorial Research Centre, Bombay, 1973, pp. 23-26.
16. *Ibid.* pp. 31-32.
17. *Ibid.*
18. Amrit Rai, *A Divided House: The Origin and Development of Hindi/Hindavi*, Oxford University Press, New Delhi, 1984, pp. 54-55.
19. See Suniti Kumar Chatterjee, *Indo-Aryan and Hindi*, Firma K.L. Mukhopadhyay, Calcutta, 1960, p. 136.

Chapter 3

1. Cited in O.P. Kejariwal, *The Asiatic Society of Bengal and the Discovery of India's Past*, Oxford University Press, New Delhi, 1988, pp. 18-19.
2. P.J. Marshall, *The British Discovery of Hinduism in the Eighteenth Century*, Cambridge University Press, Cambridge, 1970.
3. David Kopf, *British Orientalism and the Bengal Renaissance: The Dynamics of Indian Modernization 1773-1835*, University of California Press, Berkeley, 1969.
4. William Jones, 'Third Annual Discourse' (Asiatic Researches, 1788), quoted in Kopf, *op. cit.*, p. 38.
5. Quoted in Kopf, *op. cit.*, pp. 38-39.
6. *Ibid.*, p. 41.
7. John Keay, *India Discovered*, Windward (year not stated).
8. Kopf, *op. cit.*, p. 22.
9. Ronald Inden, *Imagining India*, Basil Blackwell, Oxford, 1990.
10. Adam Kuper, *The Invention of Primitive Society*, Routledge, London and New York, 1988.
11. Friedrich Max Mueller, *Indian Friends,* Indian edition, Amrit Book Company, New Delhi, 1982, p. 80.
12. David Kopf, *The Brahmo Samaj and the Shaping of the Modern Indian Mind*, Princeton University Press, Princeton, 1979, p. 265.
13. *Ibid.*, p. 266.
14. Cited in Arabinda Poddar, *Renaissance in Bengal*, Indian Institute of Advanced Study, Shimla, 1977, p. 73.
15. Sri Aurobindo, *Bankim-Tilak-Dayanand*, Sri Aurobindo Ashram, Pondicherry, 1955, pp. 12-13.

16. Poddar, *op. cit.*
17. *Ibid.*, p. 70.
18. *Ibid.*, p. 71.
19. *Ibid.*
20. *The Future of India: Complete Works of Swami Vivekanand*, Vol. III, pp. 300-01, quoted in Poddar, *op. cit.*, p. 107.
21. Quoted in Poddar, *op. cit.*, p. 117.
22. *Ibid.*, p. 104.
23. *Complete Works of Swami Vivekanand*, Vol. III, pp. 220-21.
24. Sri Aurobindo, *op. cit.*, pp. 44-45.
25. Charles H. Heimsath, *Indian Nationalism and Hindu Social Reform*, Princeton University Press, Princeton, 1964.
26. *Ibid.*, p. 316.
27. While the Hindus, on the one hand, took enthusiastically to Western education, on the other, they began to demand that Hindi, in the Devnagari script, be made the court language in place of Urdu, in North India.
28. R.C. Zaehner, *Hinduism*, Oxford University Press, London, 1966, p. 173.
29. 'Gandhi As Mahatma': Gorakhpur District, Eastern UP 1921-22 in Ranajit Guha (ed.), *Subaltern Studies*, Vol. III, Oxford University Press, New Delhi, 1984.

Chapter 4

1. Andre Wink, *Al-Hind: The Making of the Indo-Islamic World*, Oxford University Press, New Delhi, 1990, pp. 112-14.
2. *Ibid.*, pp. 10-11.
3. David Pryce-Jones, *The Closed Circle*, Paladin, London, 1990.
4. *Mutazilites*: 'Those who stand aloof'; theologians belonging to the rationalist school, which introduced speculative dogmatism in Islam. *Kharijites*: 'Those who go out'; members of a group of puritanical Muslim sects during Umayyad and Abbasid times.
5. Ernest Gellner, 'Islam and Marxism: Some Comparisons' *International Affairs*, Chatham House, **67**, 1 (1991).
6. Francis Robinson, 'Islam and Muslim Separatism' in David Taylor and Malcolm Yapp (eds.), *Political Identity in South Asia*, Curzon Press, London, 1979.
7. The concept of individual inquiry and reasoning within Islamic theology, to be conducted only by those who have a religious education and are thus qualified.
8. Yousef M. Choueiri, *Islamic Fundamentalism*, Printer Publishers, London, p. 20.

9. *Ibid.*, p. 21.

10. Brian Beedham, 'Turkey: Star of Islam', *The Economist*, London, 14-20 December 1991.

11. Barry Buzan, 'New Patterns of Global Security in the 21st Century', in *International Affairs*, Chatham House, **67**, No. 3, 1991.

12. William Lind, 'Defending Western Culture', *Foreign Policy*, No. 84, New York (Fall issue), 1991.

13. The period we are concerned with, that is, the post-Mughal era, however, witnessed powerful movements seeking, fairly successfully, to purge Indian Islam of much that was specifically Indian in it.

14. Shah Waliullah of Delhi (1703-63) linked the decline of Muslim power to deviations from the teachings of the Koran. He believed that by purging Islam of non-Muslim customs and by focussing on the Koran and Hadith, the Muslims could regain their past status.

15. Respect for well-known Sufi masters and their descendants, visits to *dargahs* (tombs of saints) and related activities could be explained wholly in terms of medieval Islam. But, in India, a movement was launched against such Islamic practices by the orthodox ulema on the ground that they resembled Hindu practices. I wish to emphasize this point because it is generally ignored in our discussions.

    In this connection I would like to quote from an article by Marc Gaborieu ['A Nineteenth Century Indian "Wahhabi" Tract against the Cult of Muslim Saints: *Al-Balagh al-Mubin*', in Christian W. Toll (ed.), *Muslim Shrines in India*, Oxford University Press London, 1989]. The article discusses a short Persian tract, *Al-Balagh al-Mubin*, attributed wrongly to Shah Waliullah but written (according to Gaborieu) by an Indian Wahhabi much later. But whoever its author may have been, it was used effectively to wage war on the Sufi saint cult. Gaborieu writes that "our author puts forward one argument which is less common; it is in my view the most interesting and forms the core of the book. The worship of saints is all the more to be prohibited because it makes Muslims resemble the Hindu polytheists among whom they live" (p. 224).

    The author of *Al-Balagh al-Mubin* listed 18 practices among the followers of the saint cult to press the charge that they were no different from Hindu idol worshippers. The intention clearly was to discredit popular Islam and destroy the bridge between Hindus and Muslims.

I would also like to refer to two excellent studies on Islam in Bengal, namely, Asim Roy's, *The Islamic Syncretist Tradition in Bengal*, Princeton University Press, Princeton, 1983, and Rafiuddin Ahmed's, *The Bengal Muslims 1871-1906: A Quest for Identity*, Oxford University Press, New Delhi, 1981. Both have described the rise and prevalence of what may be called 'genuinely Indian Islam' up to the nineteenth century.

It was this form of Islam, with the saint cult as its core, that was sought to be rejected in the nineteenth century by a number of movements such as the Ahl-i-Hadith, the Tariqah-i-Muhammadiyah, the Faraizi and the Al-Taaiyuni. To call them reform movements, which is how they are generally described, is to miss their avowedly anti-Hindu orientation.

16. Yogendra Singh, *Modernization of Indian Tradition*, Thomson Press, Delhi, 1973.

17. *Ibid.*, p. 79.

18. *Ibid.*

19. Sayyid Ahmed Barelvi is a critical figure in the history of Indian Islam. He was a disciple of Abdul Aziz, the son of Shah Waliullah, father of the revivalist movement in the early eighteenth century. As such, he was a product of the Indian Islamic environment. But while Abdul Aziz declared India *dar-ul-harb* (land of war) and sought to purify Islam by purging it of Hindu practices, he did not institute *jihad* (holy war). *Jihad* was Barelvi's contribution. That is one reason why his followers are known as Wahhabis. To begin with, *jihad* was limited to the Sikh durbar on the ground, according to some Muslims writers, that while the British allowed Muslims freedom to practise their religion, the Sikhs did not. Others disagree and hold that Sayyid Ahmed limited the *jihad* to the Sikh durbar in the first instance because, in his view, it was the weaker of two and therefore easier to dispose of. The second proposition is valid, though, as it happened, Sayyid Ahmed failed to overthrow the durbar from his fastness in the Pathan territory partly because he had to spend much of his energy and resources in trying to cope with the unruly Pathans and their shifting loyalties. The British had acquiesced in the movement of men and money from their territories and in the establishment of the Wahhabi headquarters in Patna.

The *jihad* however continued even after the Wahhabis had taken over Punjab and the north-west frontier region in 1849. The Wahhabis played a significant role in the Mutiny of 1857 and the establishment of the Dar-ul-Uloom seminary in Deoband, a major centre for training ulema in the subcontinent.

20. Pakistani society, it can be argued, is no different from Indian society in respect of its linguistic plurality. But this is a superficial view. While India represents a case of *diversity in unity* and *not of unity in diversity*, as Nehru put it in disregard of the Vedic-Sanskrit foundation of Indian civilization, Pakistan is a case of *diversity in diversity*. Islam does impose a form of unity, but from above and outside.

In India's case, every major North Indian language is based on Sanskrit and all Dravidian languages have been so deeply permeated (not just influenced) by Sanskrit that it is difficult to identify concepts and practices which are not rooted in the Sanskrit-based culture. In the deepest sense of the term 'ethnicity', India has for millennia been an ethnic entity which neither the Christian nor the Muslim world has been. Again, in a fundamental sense, Punjab and Sind in present-day Pakistan have been and remain part of this Indic ethnicity.

The imposition of the state of Pakistan on its constituent units bears comparison with the imposition of the communist ideology on the Russian empire; as in the case of the latter, it is impossible to ascertain which component has been the worst sufferer. For, if in the Soviet Union's case, it is as plausible to argue (as Alexander Solzhenitsyn does) that the Russians have paid the highest price for the misadventure as it is to suggest that other ethnic groups have been sat upon, in Pakistan's case it is as legitimate to sympathize with the Punjabis for the erosion of their identity as to plead that they have treated badly the Sindhis and the Baluchis, and up to 1971, the Bangladeshis. Such an entity could not possibly define itself in terms of its past, notwithstanding all attempts by Pakistani historians of the I.H. Qureshi school to 'invent' a history for Pakistan beginning with the Muslim invasion of Sind in the eighth century. The formation of Pakistan coincided with the onset of the cold war between the West (mainly USA) and the USSR. The cold war at once helped sustain Pakistan and limit its aggressiveness. With the termination of the cold war, Pakistan must at once feel more desperate and become more intransigent in its attitude towards India. But whatever turn events take, the conclusion is inescapable that Pakistan has not been a success story in any sense of the term.

Chapter 5

1. S. Gopal, *Jawaharlal Nehru: A Biography*, Vols. I, II and III, Oxford University Press, New Delhi, 1976, 1979 and 1984.

2. *Jawaharlal Nehru's Speeches*, Vol. I, September 1946 to May 1949, Publications Division, Government of India, New Delhi, 1963, pp. 335-37.
3. *Ibid.*, Vol. II, August 1949 to February 1953, 1983, pp. 357-59.
4. *Ibid.*, Vol. IV, September 1957 to April 1963, 1983, p.3.

Chapter 6

1. Jagmohan, *My Frozen Turbulence in Kashmir*, Allied Publishers, New Delhi, 1991, p. 138.
2. On the face of it, the contest has been, and is, between 'communalist' Hindus, who equate Hinduism with nationalism and 'secularist' Hindus who believe that India has been, and is, larger than Hinduism. In reality the picture has been made more complicated inasmuch as 'secular' nationalism in India has been underwritten, at least partly, by casteism. All parties have been fairly attentive to 'caste arithmetic'. The competition, as a shrewd Congress leader once said to me, has been between 'communalism' and 'casteism'.

Appendix 1

1. Srikant G. Telageri, *Aryan Invasion Theory and Indian Nationalism*, Voice of India, New Delhi, 1993.
2. David Frawley, *Gods, Sages and Kings: Vedic Secrets of Ancient Civilization*, Indian edn. Motilal Banarssidass, New Delhi.

Appendix 2

1. Gai Eaton, *Islam and the Destiny of Man*, George Allen and Unwin, London, 1985.

Index